PEGASUS BRIDGE
6 June 1944

PEGASUS BRIDGE

6 June 1944

Stephen E. Ambrose

London
GEORGE ALLEN & UNWIN
Sydney

George Allen & Unwin (Publishers) Ltd,
40 Museum Street, London WC1A 1LU, UK

George Allen & Unwin (Publishers) Ltd,
Park Lane, Hemel Hempstead, Herts HP2 4TE, UK

George Allen & Unwin Australia Pty Ltd,
8 Napier Street, North Sydney, NSW 2060, Australia

ISBN 0 04 923076 X

Set in 11 on 12 point Plantin by Nene Phototypesetters Ltd, Northampton
and printed in Great Britain by Biddles Ltd, Guildford, Surrey

For Den Brotheridge

Contents

Introduction

This book is the result of some 24 interviews, conducted between September and December, 1983, in Canada, England, France and Germany. At that time I had just completed some twenty years of work on Dwight Eisenhower, during which period I examined something over two million documents. In my next book I wanted to work from an entirely different kind of source material. I have always been impressed by the work of the American military writer S. L. A. Marshall, especially by his use of post-combat interviews to determine what actually happened on the battlefield.

My thought was, Why not do a post-combat interview forty years after the event? Even taking into account all the tricks that memory plays, I felt that for many of the participants, D-Day was the great day of their lives, stamped forever in their memories. I knew that was the case with Eisenhower, who went on to two full terms as President, but who always looked back on D-Day as his greatest day, and could remember the most surprising details. I also wanted to come down from the dizzying heights of the Supreme Commander and the President to the company level, where the action is. Further, I wanted a company that was unusual and that played a crucial role, Pegasus Bridge was an obvious choice.

So I set out. My recorded interviews with John Howard took twenty hours, spread over a period of some weeks. I got almost ten hours of tape from Jim Wallwork. My shortest interview was two hours.

Listening to the old veterans was fascinating. D-Day had indeed burned itself indelibly into their minds, and they very much enjoyed having an interested audience for their stories.

My major problem, it turned out, was the sequence and timing of events: I sometimes got six, eight, or ten individual descriptions of the same incident. When the veterans differed it was only in small detail, but they often disagreed on when the specific incident took place, whether before this one or after that one. By comparing all the transcripts later, by using such documentary material as exists, and by constant re-checking with my sources, I worked out a sequence of events and incidents that is, I think, as close to accurate as one can get forty years later.

The key time, on which everything else hinges, is the moment the first glider crashed. I use 0016, D-Day, as that moment. That was the time at which John Howard's watch, and the watch of one of the privates, both stopped – presumably as a result of the crash.

When I began writing the book I quickly realised that the more these men and women spoke for themselves, the better. I found myself using more and longer quotations than I had ever used before. Gradually, I realised that what I was doing was putting their stories into a single narrative, rather than writing my own book. Because this is, truly, a book written by the veterans themselves, I'm glad to say that the royalties are going to the Royal Greenjackets Consolidated Charitable Fund (the Oxfordshire and Buckinghamshire Light Infantry became the 1st Battalion of the Royal Greenjackets in the late 1950s).

The informants (listed in the order the interviews were done)

Jim Wallwork, John Howard, Wally Parr, Dennis Fox, Richard Todd, Nigel Poett, Nigel Taylor, M. Thornton, Oliver Boland, C. Hooper, E. Tappenden, Henry Hickman and Billy Gray (a joint interview), David Wood, John Vaughan, R. Ambrose, Jack Bailey, Joy Howard, Irene Parr, R. Smith, H. Sweeney, E. O'Donnell, Thérèse Gondrée, and Hans von Luck.

Prologue

SPRING, 1944

The spring of 1944 was a unique time in European history, unique because virtually every European was anticipating a momentous event. That event was the Allied invasion, and everyone knew that it would decide whether the continent lived under Nazi domination.

By May of that year the war had reached its decisive phase, a phase in which invasion was inevitable. The British had been planning to return to Europe since they were kicked off in 1940. The Russians had been demanding the opening of a second front since the June of 1941, insisting that the Germans could never be beaten without one. And the Americans had been in agreement with the Russians since their entry into the war. Generals George Marshall and Dwight D. Eisenhower had argued forcefully for a second front in 1942 and 1943.

Despite the commitment by the three great allies, and despite intense public pressure, another strategy was followed. In November, 1942, the Allies landed in French North Africa, a long way from any major German forces (not to mention from any German cities). In July of the following year they landed in Sicily, and two months later in southern Italy. These operations ran into heavy German opposition, but they did not put a significant strain on enemy manpower. Nor did they seriously weaken Germany's capacity to make war: indeed, German factories were producing tanks and guns at record rates by the spring of 1944. And their guns and tanks were the best in the world – as well they might be, given the Nazis' ability to draw on the expertise and resources of all Europe. In short, the Allied operations in the Mediterranean during 1942 and 1943 were more important for their political than their military results. They left Hitler with few problems either of production or of manpower.

But Hitler did have one major worry in the Spring of 1944, and that was a single point at which his fighting forces were vulnerable. He was well protected on the north, where his troops occupied Norway and Denmark. To the south, the immense barrier of the Alps stood between Germany and the Allied forces, who in any case were still south of Rome. Hitler was not even excessively worried about his eastern flank: his armies were 600 miles east of Warsaw, and within 300 miles of Moscow. He had lost the Ukraine in 1943, much his biggest loss to date, but for compensation he had held on in the Balkans and was still besieging Leningrad. On all fronts except one he had a deep buffer between himself and his enemies. That one exception was to the west.

The Allied forces building up in the United Kingdom, now 2,500,000 strong, were the greatest threat to Cologne and Germany's industrial heartland. Not only were they much closer than the Red Army, they were operating from a virtually impregnable base and had far greater mobility than either the German or Russian armies. But of course there was the English Channel between Hitler's Europe and the armies gathering in the United Kingdom. Hitler knew, from intensive study of the plans for operation Sea Lion, a German invasion of Britain in 1940, just how difficult a cross-Channel attack would be.

Hitler did what he could to make it even more difficult. Just as the British started thinking about returning to the Continent even as they were leaving Dunkirk, so did Hitler begin thinking then of how to repulse an invasion. First the ports were fortified, protected by big guns on the cliffs, by machine-gun emplacements, by trenches, by mine fields and barbed wire, by underwater obstacles, by every device known to German engineers. The Canadians learned how effective these were at Dieppe in August, 1942, when they were met by a veritable wall of steel hurtling down on them from every direction. In 1943, the Germans began extending the fortifications up and down the coast; in January, 1944, with Rommel's arrival to take command of Army Group B, construction reached an almost frenzied pace. The Germans knew that the second front had to come that spring, and that throwing the invaders back was their single best chance to win the war.

Hitler had therefore turned a staggering amount of labour and material, taken from all over Europe, to the construction of the Atlantic Wall. All along the French and Belgian coasts, but especially between Ostend and Cherbourg, the Germans had built or were building machine-gun pillboxes, trenches, observation posts, artillery emplacements, fortresses, mine fields, flooded fields, underwater obstacles of every conceivable type, a communications network. This was a regular Maginot Line, only much longer – truly a gigantic undertaking unprecedented in Western history, and comparable only to the Great Wall of China.

If Eisenhower's forces could break through that Wall, victory was not assured, but it was at least possible and even probable. If they could not get ashore, their chances were doubtful. Eisenhower said it well in his first report to the Combined Chiefs of Staff: 'Every obstacle must be overcome, every inconvenience suffered and every risk run to ensure that our blow is decisive. We cannot afford to fail.'

To meet the challenge, the United States, Great Britain, and Canada all turned the greater part of their energies to the task of launching an assault and establishing a beach-head. Their venture was code-named Operation Overlord; nearly every citizen of the three nations involved made a direct personal contribution to launching it.

As a consequence, Eisenhower's problems did not include a shortage of material. He had an abundant supply of tanks, guns, trucks. His problem was how to get them across the Channel and into battle. The tanks and heavy artillery could only be brought ashore gradually, especially on D-Day itself and for a few days after that. Thus, the Allied forces would be at their most vulnerable after the first wave had landed and before the follow-up waves got ashore with their tanks and guns. The troops themselves would be heavily outnumbered (by as much as ten to one) in the first days of the invasion, and as late as

D-Day plus one month the ratio would be five to one. But many of the German divisions, fifty-five in all, were scattered all across France; many were immobile, and many were of low quality. Furthermore, Eisenhower could count on the Allied air forces to keep German movement to a minimum, at least in daylight. And he had chosen as the invasion site the area west of the Orne River: this avoided the bulk of German strength in France, which was north and east of the mouth of the Seine. In that area, and most of all around the Pas de Calais, German defences were strongest. In addition, the Germans had most of their panzer strength in the Pas de Calais.

Because the panzers were to the east, the most dangerous flank of the invasion for the Allies was the left flank. It was closest to the major German counter-attack formations and therefore the place where Eisenhower expected the most determined – and most dangerous – counter-attacks.

For immediate counter-attack purposes, Rommel had two armoured divisions, the 12th SS Panzer and the 21st Panzer, stationed in and to the east of Caen. Eisenhower's greatest fear was that Rommel would send those divisions, operating as a coordinated unit, on a counter-attack against his left flank, code-named Sword Beach, just west of the mouth of the Orne River. It was possible that those two panzer divisions would drive the British 3rd Infantry Division on Sword back into the sea. It was also possible that, on D-Day plus one or two, additional panzer divisions would come into Normandy to participate in flank attacks along the beaches. They would strike first against Juno, then Gold, and finally the American beaches at Omaha and Utah. With fighting going on along the beaches, all Eisenhower's loading schedules would be disrupted.

To prevent such a catastrophe, Eisenhower expected to delay and harass the German tanks moving into Normandy by using the Allied air force, which had complete command of the air. The trouble was that the air forces could not operate either at night or in bad weather. By themselves, they would not be able to isolate the battlefield. Eisenhower needed some additional way to protect Sword Beach and his critical left flank.

To solve his problem, Eisenhower turned to another of the assets that Allied control of the air made available to him – airborne forces, extraordinarily mobile and elite units. German success with paratroopers and gliderborne troops in the first years of World War II had convinced the British and American armies of the need to create their own airborne divisions. Now Eisenhower had four such divisions available to him, the US 82nd and 101st Airborne and the British 1st and 6th Airborne. He decided to use them on his flanks: offensively to provide immediate tactical assistance by seizing bridges, road junctions, and the like; defensively to keep the Germans occupied and confused. The British 6th Airborne, dropping east of Sword Beach, had another critical task: setting up a blocking force to keep the German panzers away from the left flank.

Critical though those tasks were, they did not seem critical enough to George C. Marshall, the US Army Chief of Staff. Marshall was so strongly opposed to Eisenhower's plan that he sent Eisenhower what amounted to a reprimand – and was certainly the most critical letter he ever wrote to his protégé. Marshall's criticism, and Eisenhower's response, bring out very clearly the advantages and disadvantages of airborne troops.

Marshall pointed out that the role assigned to the airborne forces was basically defensive, and stated flatly that he did not like the concept at all. No attempt was being made to engage or disrupt the enemy's strategic forces or counter-attack capability. Marshall told Eisenhower that when he was creating the 82nd and 101st, he had had great hopes for paratroopers as a new element in warfare, but he confessed that his hopes had not been realised, and now Eisenhower's plans made him despair. Marshall saw in the plan a wasteful dispersion of three elite divisions, with two American on the right protecting Utah's flank and one British on the left protecting Sword's flank. He charged that there had been a 'lack in conception' caused by a piecemeal approach, with General Omar Bradley insisting that he had to have paratrooper help at Utah and General Bernard Law Montgomery insisting that Sword Beach also had to have paratrooper aid.

This business of splitting up the paratroopers was all a mistake, Marshall told Eisenhower. If he were in command of Overlord, he would insist on one large paratrooper operation, 'even to the extent that should the British be in opposition I would carry it out exclusively with American troops'. He would make the drop south of Evreux, nearly seventy-five miles inland from Caen. There were four good airfields near Evreux which could be quickly taken, making re-supply possible. 'This plan appeals to me', Marshall declared, 'because I feel that it is a true vertical envelopment and would create such a strategic threat to the Germans that it would call for a major revision of their defensive plans.' Bradley's and Montgomery's flanks could take care of themselves, in short, because the German tanks would be busy attacking the airborne troops around Evreux. Such a massive drop would be a complete surprise, would directly threaten both the crossings of the Seine and Paris, and would serve as a rallying point for the French Resistance.

The only drawback Marshall could see to his plan was 'that we have never done anything like this before, and frankly, that reaction makes me tired'. The Chief of Staff concluded by saying that he did not want to put undue pressure on Eisenhower, but did want to make sure that Eisenhower at least considered the possibility of making a bolder, more effective strategic use of his airborne troops.

Eisenhower's reply was long and defensive. He said that for more than a year one of his favourite subjects for contemplation had been getting ahead of the enemy in some important method of operation, and the strategic use of paratroopers was an obvious possibility. Marshall's idea, however, was impossible. First, Eisenhower insisted that Bradley and Montgomery were right: the flanks of the invasion had to be protected from German armoured counter-attacks. Second, and even more important, a paratrooper force three divisions strong landing seventy-five miles inland would not be self-contained, would lack mobility and heavy fire-power, and would therefore be destroyed. The Germans had shown time and again that they did not fear a 'strategic threat of envelopment'. Using the road net of France, Rommel could concentrate immense firepower against an isolated force and defeat it in detail.

Eisenhower cited the Allied experience at Anzio early in 1944 as an example. They had landed there in an attempt to slip around the German line in Italy, thereby threatening both the rear of the German line and Rome itself. Eisenhower told Marshall that 'any military man required to analyse' the situation in Italy right after the Anzio landing 'would have said that the only hope of the German was to begin the instant and rapid withdrawal of his troops'. Instead the Germans attacked, and because the Anzio force did not have enough tanks and trucks to provide mobile striking power, the Allies barely held out. And they held out, Eisenhower emphasised, only because the Allies had command of the sea and could provide support in both material and gunfire directly onto the beachhead. An inland airborne force would be cut off from all but air supply, which could not provide enough tanks, trucks, heavy artillery, or bulldozers and other equipment to withstand German armoured attacks. It would be annihilated.

Eisenhower was unwilling to take the risk Marshall proposed. He believed that paratroopers dropped near Evreux would not be a strategic threat to the Germans, that indeed they would just be paratroopers wasted, and might even be made a hostage, just as the Anzio force had become. 'I instinctively dislike ever to uphold the conservative as opposed to the bold', Eisenhower concluded, but he would not change his plans. Marshall did not raise the subject again.

Nothing like Marshall's plan was ever tried. At Arnhem, in September, 1944, three airborne divisions were used, but they were dropped many miles apart with separate objectives. Therefore we cannot know who was correct, Eisenhower or Marshall. But Eisenhower was in command, so it was his plan – admittedly conservative rather than bold – that was used.

Thus did the British 6th Airborne Division get its D-Day assignment. The task of carrying out that assignment fell to General Richard Gale, commander of the 6th Airborne. Gale decided to drop his division east of the Orne River, about five to seven miles inland, in the low ground between the Orne and the River Dives. The main body would gather in and around the village of Ranville, and would guard the bridges over the Orne

Canal and River. Specially-trained companies would capture and destroy the four bridges over the River Dives, then fall back on Ranville; others would destroy the German battery at Merville.

Central to Gale's plan was taking and holding the bridges over the Orne waterways, without which the 6th Airborne would be unable to receive tanks, trucks, and other equipment from the beaches. They were critical to the success of the whole invasion, and the operation to take and hold them would require meticulous planning, rigorous training, and bold execution.

That operation is the subject of this book.

CHAPTER ONE

D-Day: 0000 to 0015 hours

It was a steel girder bridge, painted grey, with a large water tower and superstructure. At 0000 hours, June 5/6, 1944, the scudding clouds parted sufficiently to allow the nearly-full moon to shine and reveal the bridge, standing starkly visible above the shimmering water of the Caen Canal.

On the bridge, Private Vern Bonck, a twenty-two-year-old Pole conscripted into the German army, clicked his heels sharply as he saluted Private Helmut Romer, a sixteen-year-old Berliner who had reported to relieve him. As Bonck went off duty, he met with his fellow sentry, another Pole. They decided they were not sleepy and agreed to go to the local brothel, in the village of Benouville, for a bit of fun. They strolled west along the bridge road, then turned south at the T junction, on the road into Benouville. By 0005 they were at the brothel, and within minutes they were knocking back cheap red wine with two French prostitutes.

Beside the bridge, on the west bank, south of the road, Georges and Thérèse Gondrée and their two daughters slept in their small café. Georges and Thérèse were in separate rooms, not by choice but as a way to use every room and thus to keep the Germans from billeting soldiers with them. It was the 1,450th night of the German occupation of Benouville.

So far as the Germans knew, the Gondrées were simple Norman peasants, people of no consequence who gave them no trouble. Indeed, Georges sold beer, coffee, food, and a concoction made by Madame of rotting melons and half-fermented sugar, to the grateful German troops stationed at the

1

bridge. There were about fifty of them, the NCOs and officers all German, the enlisted men mostly conscripts from East Europe.

But the Gondrées were not as simple as they pretended to be. Madame came from Alsace and spoke German, a fact she successfully hid from the garrison. Georges, before acquiring the café, had spent twelve years as a clerk in Lloyd's Bank in Paris and spoke English. Both hated the Germans for what they had done to France, hated the life they led under the occupation, feared for the future of their eight-year-old daughter, and were consequently active in trying to bring German rule to an end. In their case, the most valuable thing they could do for the Allies was to provide information on conditions at the bridge. Thérèse got information by listening to the chit-chat of the NCOs in the café; she passed what she heard along to Georges, who passed it to Madame Vion, director of the maternity hospital, who passed it along to the Resistance in Caen on her trips to obtain medical supplies. From Caen, the information was passed onto England via Lysander aeroplanes, small craft that could land in fields and get out in a hurry.

Only a few days before, on June 2, Georges had sent through this process a titbit Thérèse had overheard – that the button that would set off the explosives to blow the bridge was located in the machine-gun pillbox across the road from the anti-tank gun. He hoped that information had got through, if only because he would hate to see his bridge destroyed.

The man who would give that order, the commander of the garrison at the bridge, was Major Hans Schmidt. Schmidt had an understrength company of the 736th Grenadier Regiment of the 716th Infantry Division. At 0000 hours, June 5/6, he was in Ranville, a village two kilometres east of the Orne River. The river ran parallel to the canal, about 400 metres to the east, and was also crossed by a bridge (fixed, and guarded by sentries but without emplacements or a garrison). The Germans knew that the long-anticipated invasion could come at any time, and Schmidt had been told that the two bridges were the most critical points in Normandy because they provided the only crossings of the Orne waterways along the Norman coast road.

Nonetheless, Schmidt did not have his garrison at full alert; nor was he in Ranville on business. Except for the two sentries on each bridge, his troops were either sleeping in their bunkers, or dozing in their slit trenches or in the machine-gun pillbox, or enjoying themselves at the Benouville brothel.

Schmidt himself was with his girlfriend in Ranville, enjoying the magnificent food and drink of Normandy. He thought of himself as a fanatical Nazi, someone who was determined to do his duty for his Führer, but he seldom let duty interfere with pleasure, and he had no worries that evening. His routine concern was the possibility that French partisans might blow the bridges, but that hardly seemed likely except in conjunction with an airborne operation, and the high winds and stormy weather of the past two days precluded a parachute drop. Having received orders to blow the bridges himself if capture seemed imminent, he had prepared the bridges for demolition. But he had not put the explosives into their chambers, for fear of accident or the partisans. As his bridges were almost five miles inland, Schmidt reckoned he would have plenty of warning before any Allied units reached him, even para-troopers, because the paras were notorious for taking a long time to form up and get organised after their drops scattered them all over the DZ. Thus, tonight Schmidt could relax. He treated himself to more wine, and another pinch.

At Vimont, east of Caen, Colonel Hans A. von Luck, com-manding the 125th Panzer Grenadier Regiment of the 21st Panzer Division, was working on personnel reports at his headquarters. The contrast between Schmidt and von Luck extended far beyond their activities at midnight. Schmidt had gone soft from years of cushy occupation duty; von Luck was an officer hardened by combat. He had been in Poland in 1939 and commanded the leading reconnaissance battalion for Rommel at Dunkirk in 1940. At Moscow in the winter of 1941, he actually led his battalion into the outskirts of the city, the deepest penetration of the campaign. And he had been with Rommel throughout the North African campaign of 1942–43.

There was an equally sharp contrast between the units

von Luck and Schmidt commanded. The 716th Infantry was a second-rate, poorly equipped, immobile division made up of a hotchpotch of Poles, Russian, French and other conscripted troops, while the 21st Panzer was Rommel's favourite division. Von Luck's regiment, the 125th, was one of the best equipped in the German army. The 21st Panzer Division had been destroyed in Tunisia in April and May, 1943, but Rommel had got most of the officer corps out of the trap, and around that nucleus rebuilt the division. It had all new equipment, including Tiger tanks, self-propelled vehicles (SPV) of all types, and an outstanding wireless communications network. The men were volunteers, young Germans deliberately raised by the Nazis for the challenge they were about to face, tough, well-trained, eager to come to grips with the enemy.

There was a tremendous amount of air activity that night, with British and American bombers crossing the Channel to bomb Caen. As usual, Schmidt paid no attention to it. Neither did von Luck, consciously, but he was so accustomed to the sights and sounds of combat that at about 0010 hours he noticed something none of his clerks did. There were about six planes flying unusually low, at 500 feet or less. That could only mean they were dropping something by parachute. Probably supplies for the Resistance, von Luck thought; he ordered a search of the area, hoping to capture some local resistance people while they were gathering in the supplies.

Heinrich (now Henry) Heinz Hickman, a sergeant in the German 6th (Independent) Parachute Regiment, was at that moment riding in an open staff car, coming from Ouistreham on the coast towards Benouville. Hickman, twenty-four years old, was a combat veteran of Sicily and Italy. His regiment had come to Normandy a fortnight before; at 2300 hours on June 5 his company commander had ordered Hickman to pick up four young privates at observation posts outside Ouistreham and bring them back to headquarters, near Breville on the east side of the river.

Hickman, himself a paratrooper, also had heard low-flying planes. He came to the same conclusion as von Luck, that they were dropping supplies to the Resistance, and for the same reason – he could not imagine that the Allies would make a paratrooper drop with only half-dozen sticks. He drove on towards the bridge over the Caen Canal.

Over the Channel, at 0000 hours, two groups of three Halifax bombers flew at 7,000 feet towards Caen. With all the other air activity going on, neither German searchlights nor AA gunners noticed that each Halifax was tugging a Horsa glider.

Inside the lead glider, Private Wally Parr of D Company, the 2nd Oxfordshire and Buckinghamshire Light Infantry (Ox and Bucks), a part of the Air Landing Brigade of the 6th Airborne Division of the British army, was leading the twenty-eight men in singing. With his powerful voice and strong Cockney accent, Parr was booming out 'Abey, Abey, My Boy'. Billy Gray, sitting down the row from Parr, was barely singing, because all that he could think about was the 'Jimmy Riddle' he had to do. At the back of the glider, Corporal Jack Bailey sang even as he worried about the parachute he was responsible for securing.

The pilot, twenty-four-year-old Staff Sergeant Jim Wallwork, of the Glider Pilot Regiment, anticipated casting off any second now that he had seen the surf breaking over the Norman coast. Beside him his co-pilot, Staff Sergeant John Ainsworth, was concentrating intensely on his stop watch. Sitting behind Ainsworth, the commander of D Company, Major John Howard, a thirty-one-year-old former sergeant major and an ex-cop, laughed with everyone else when the song ended and Parr called out, 'Has the Major laid his kit yet?' Howard suffered from air sickness and had vomited on every training flight. This flight, however, was an exception. Like his men, he had not been in combat before, but the prospect seemed to calm him more than it shook him.

As Parr started up 'It's a Long Way to Tipperary', Howard touched the tiny red shoe in his battlejacket pocket, one of his two-year-old son Terry's infant shoes that he had brought along for good luck. He thought of Joy, his wife, and of Terry and their baby daughter, Penny. They were back in Oxford, living near a factory, and he hoped there were no bombing raids that night. Beside Howard sat Lieutenant Den Brotheridge, whose

5

wife was pregnant and due to deliver any day (five other men in the company had pregnant wives back in England). Howard had talked Brotheridge into joining the Ox and Bucks, and had selected his platoon for the no. 1 glider because he thought Brotheridge and his platoon about the best in his company. Another reason was that they were mostly Londoners like himself. Howard loved the Cockney quick wit and cheerfulness.

One minute behind Wallwork's glider was no. 2, carrying Lieutenant David Wood's platoon. Another minute behind that Horsa was no. 3 glider, with Lieutenant R. A. A. 'Sandy' Smith's platoon. The three gliders in this group were going to cross the coast near Cabourg, well east of the mouth of the Orne River.

Parallel to that group, to the west and a few minutes behind, Captain Brian Priday sat with Lieutenant Tony Hooper's platoon, followed by the gliders carrying the platoons of Lieutenants H. J. 'Tod' Sweeney and Dennis Fox. This second group was headed towards the mouth of the Orne River. In Fox's platoon, Sergeant M. C. 'Wagger' Thornton was singing 'Cow Cow Boogie' and – like almost everyone else on all the gliders – chain-smoking Player's cigarettes.

In no. 2 glider, with the first group, the pilot, Staff Sergeant Oliver Boland, who had just turned twenty-three a fortnight before, found crossing the Channel an 'enormously emotional' experience, setting off as he was 'as the spearhead of the most colossal army ever assembled. I found it difficult to believe because I felt so insignificant.'

At 0007, Wallwork cast off his lead glider as he crossed the coast. At that instant, the invasion had begun. There were 156,000 men prepared to go into France that day, by air and by sea, British, Canadian, and American, organised into some 12,000 companies. D Company led the way. It was not only the spearhead of the mighty host, it was also the only company attacking as a completely independent unit. Howard would have no one to report to, or take orders from, until he had completed his principal task. When Wallwork cast off, D Company was on its own.

With castoff there was a sudden jerk, then dead silence.

Parr and his singers shut up, the engine noise of the bomber faded away, and there was a silence broken only by the swoosh of air over the Horsa's wings. Clouds covered the moon; Ainsworth had to use a torch to see his stop watch, which he had started instantaneously with castoff.

After casting off the Halifax bombers continued on towards Caen, where they were to drop their small bomb load on the cement factory, more as a diversion than a serious attack. During the course of the campaign, Caen was almost completely obliterated, with hardly a brick left mortared to a brick. The only untouched building in the whole city was the cement factory. 'They were great tug pilots', says Wallwork, 'but terrible bombers.'

Howard's thoughts shifted from Joy, Terry and Penny to his other 'family', D Company. He thought of how deeply involved he was with his platoon commanders, his sergeants and corporals, and many of his privates. They had been preparing for this moment, together, for over two years. The officers and men had done all that he asked of them, and more. By God, they were the best damn company in the whole British army! They had earned this extraordinary role, they deserved it. John was proud of every one of them, and of himself, and he felt a wave of comradeship come over him, and he loved them all.

Then his mind flashed through the dangers ahead. The anti-glider poles, first of all – air reconnaissance photographs taken in the past few days revealed that the Germans were digging holes for the poles (called 'Rommel's asparagus' by the Allies). Were the poles in place, or not? Everything depended on the pilots until the instant the glider had landed, and until that instant Howard was but a passenger. If the pilots could bring D Company down, safely, within 400 metres of the objective, he was confident he could carry out his first task successfully. But if the pilots were even one kilometre off course, he doubted that he could do his job. Anything over a kilometre and there was no chance. If the Germans somehow spotted the gliders coming in, and got a machine-gun on them, the men would never touch the soil of France alive. If the pilots crashed – into a tree, an embankment, or one of Rommel's

7

asparagus – they might all well die even if their feet did touch ground.

Howard was always a bad passenger; he always wanted to drive himself. On this occasion, as he willed Wallwork onto the target, he at least had something physical to do for diversion. Held by Howard on one side and the platoon sergeant on the other, Lieutenant Brotheridge released his safety belt and leaned forward to open the door in front of them. The door slid up into the roof of the glider and Brotheridge accomplished this in one hefty swoop. It was a dicey business because Howard and Sergeant Ollis were hanging on to Brotheridge's equipment, and when the job was done, Brotheridge slumped back into his seat with a sigh of relief.

Looking down, once the door was open, the men could see nothing but cloud. Still they grinned at each other, recalling the fifty-franc bet they had made as to who would be the first out of the glider.

As Brotheridge took his seat again, Howard's orders flashed through his mind. Dated May 2, they were signed by Brigadier Nigel Poett and classified 'Bigot', a super-classification above 'Top Secret'. (The few who did have clearance for 'Bigot' material were said to be 'bigoted'.)

> 'Your task is to seize *intact* the bridges over the River Orne and canal at Benouville and Ranville, and to hold them until relief. . . . The capture of the bridges will be a *coup de main* operation depending largely on surprise, speed and dash for success. Provided the bulk of your force lands safely, you should have little difficulty in overcoming the known opposition on the bridges. Your difficulties will arise in holding off an enemy counter-attack on the bridges, until you are relieved.'

The relief would come from the men of the 6th Airborne Division, specifically from the 5th Para Brigade and especially its 7th Battalion. They would land in DZs between the Orne River and the River Dives at 0050 hours, roughly half an hour after Howard's party. Brigadier Poett, commanding 5th Para Brigade, told Howard that he could expect organised reinforcements within two hours of touchdown. The paras would come through Ranville, where Poett intended to set up his Brigade headquarters for the defence of the bridges.

Poett himself was only two or three minutes behind Howard, flying with the pathfinders who would mark the DZ for the main body of the 5th Para Brigade. There were six planes in Poett's group – the low-flying planes von Luck and Hickman had heard. Poett wanted to be the first to jump, but at 0008 hours he was struggling desperately to get the floor hatch open. He and his ten men were jammed into an old Albemarle bomber, which none of them had ever seen before. They were carrying so much equipment that they had to 'push and push and push to get in'. They had then had a terrible time squeezing together sufficiently to close the hatch door. Now, over the Channel with the coast coming up, they could not get the damn thing open. Poett began to fear he would never get out at all, that he would end up landing ignominiously back in England.

In no. 3 glider, Lieutenant Sandy Smith felt his stomach clinch as it did before a big sports event. He was only twenty-two years old, and he rather liked the feeling of tension, because he was full of the confidence he used to feel before a match when he was a Cambridge rugger blue. 'We were eager', he remembers, 'we were fit. And we were totally innocent. I mean my idea was that everyone was going to be incredibly brave with drums beating and bands playing and I was going to be the bravest among the brave. There was absolutely no doubt at all in my mind that that was going to be the case.'

Across the aisle from Smith, Captain John Vaughan of the Royal Army Medical Corps sat fidgeting. He was distinctly unhappy when Smith opened the door. Vaughan was a doctor with the paratroopers, had many jumps behind him, had confidence in a parachute. But he had volunteered for this special mission, not knowing what it was, and ended up in a plywood glider, an open door in front of him, and no parachute. He kept thinking, 'My God, why haven't I got a parachute?'

Back in Oxford, Joy Howard slept. She had had a routine day, taking care of Terry and Penny, getting them into bed at 7 p.m., doing her housework, then spending a couple of hours by the radio, smocking Penny's little dresses.

9

On his last furlough, John had hidden his service dress uniform in a spare room closet. He had then taken Terry's shoe, kissed the children, started to leave, and returned to kiss them once more. As he left, he told Joy that when she heard that the invasion had started, she could stop worrying, because his job would be finished. Joy had discovered the missing shoe and found the uniform. She knew that the invasion must be imminent, because leaving the uniform behind meant that John did not expect to be dining in the officers' mess for the foreseeable future.

But that had been weeks ago, and nothing had happened since. For two years there had been talk of an invasion, but nothing happened. On June 5, 1944, Joy had no special feelings – she just went to bed. She did hear air traffic, but because most of the bombers based in the Midlands were headed south, rather than east, she was on the fringes of the great air armada and paid little attention to the accustomed noise. She slept.

Down in the southeastern end of London, almost in Kent, Irene Parr did hear and see the huge air fleet headed towards Normandy and she immediately surmised that the invasion had begun, partly because of the numbers, partly because Wally – in a gross breach of security – had told her that D Company was going to lead the way, and he guessed it would be in the first week of June, when the moon was right. She did not know, of course, exactly where he was, but she was sure he was in great danger, and prayed for him. She would have been pleased, had she known, that Wally's last thoughts, before leaving England, were of her. Just before boarding Wallwork's Horsa, Wally had taken a piece of chalk and christened the glider the 'Lady Irene'.

Wallwork had crossed the coast well to the east of the mouth of the Orne River. Although he was the pilot of the no. 1 glider, and nos. 2 and 3 were directly behind him, he was not leading the group to the LZ – the Landing Zone. Rather, each pilot was on his own, as the pilots could not see the other gliders in any case. Boland remembers the feeling 'of being on your own up there, dead quiet, floating over the coast of France, and knowing that there's no turning back'.

Wallwork could not see the bridges, not even the river and canal. He was flying by Ainsworth's stop-watch, watching his compass, his airspeed indicator, his altimeter. Three minutes and forty-two seconds into the run, Ainsworth said, 'Now!', and Wallwork threw the descending glider into a full right turn.

He looked out the window for a landmark. He could see nothing. 'I can't see the Bois de Bavent', he whispered to Ainsworth, not wanting to upset his passengers. Ainsworth snapped back, 'For God's sake, Jim, it's the biggest place in Normandy. Pay attention.'

'It's not there', Jim whispered fiercely.

'Well, we are on course anyway', Ainsworth replied. Then he started counting: '5, 4, 3, 2, 1, Bingo. Right one turn to starboard onto course'. Wallwork heaved over the wooden steering wheel and executed another turn. He was now headed north, along the east bank of the canal, descending rapidly. Using the extra large 'barn door' wing flaps, he had brought the glider from 7,000 to about 500 feet, and reduced her airspeed from 160 mph to about 110 mph.

Below and behind him, Caen was ablaze with tracers, searchlights, and fires started by the bombers. Ahead of him, he could see nothing. He hoped that Ainsworth was right and they were on target.

That target was a small, triangular field, about 500 metres long, with the base on the south, the tip near the south-east end of the canal bridge. Wallwork could not see it, but he had studied photographs and a detailed model of the area so long and so hard that he had a vivid mental picture of what he was headed towards.

There was the bridge itself, with its superstructure and water tower at the east end the dominant feature of the flat landscape. There was a machine-gun pillbox just north of the bridge, on the east side, and an anti-tank gun emplacement across the road from it. These fortifications were surrounded by barbed wire. At Wallwork's last briefing with Howard, Howard had told him that he wanted the nose of the Horsa to break through the barbed wire, which otherwise would need to be destroyed with bangalore torpedoes. Wallwork thought to himself that there was not a chance in hell that he could land that heavy,

11

cumbersome, badly overloaded, powerless Horsa with such precision over a bumpy and untested landing strip he could barely see. But out loud he assured Howard he would do his best. What he and Ainsworth thought, however, was that such a sudden stop would result in 'a broken leg or so, maybe two each'. And they agreed amongst themselves that if they got out of this caper with only broken legs, they would be lucky.

Along with the constant concern about his location, and with the intense effort to penetrate the darkness and clouds, Wallwork had other worries. He would be doing between 90 and 100 mph when he hit the ground. If he ran into a tree, or an anti-glider pole, he would be dead, his passengers too injured or stunned to carry out their task. And the parachute worried him, too. It was in the back of the glider, held in place by Corporal Bailey. Wallwork had agreed to add the parachute at the last minute, because his Horsa was so overloaded and Howard refused to remove one more round of ammunition. The idea was that the arrester parachute would provide a safer, quicker stop. Wallwork feared that it would throw him into a nose-dive.

The control mechanism for the chute was over Ainsworth's head. At the proper moment, he would press an electric switch and the trapdoor would fall open, the chute billow out. When Ainsworth pressed another switch, the chute would fall away from the glider. Wallwork understood the theory; he just hoped he would not have to use the chute in fact.

At 0014 Wallwork called over his shoulder to Howard to get ready. Howard and the men linked arms and brought their knees up, following normal landing drill. Everyone knew the floor of the glider would disintegrate on landing. Most everyone thought the obvious thoughts – 'No turning back now', or 'Here we go', or 'This is it'. Howard recalled, 'I could see ole Jim holding that bloody great machine and driving it in at the last minute, the look on his face was one that one could never forget. I could see those damn great footballs of sweat across his forehead and all over his face.'

Gliders 2 and 3 were directly behind Wallwork, at their one-minute intervals. The other group of Horsas was, however, now split up. Priday's no. 4 glider had gone up the River Dives rather than the Orne River. Seeing a bridge over the Dives at about the right distance inland, the pilot of no. 4 glider was preparing to land. The other two Horsas, on the correct course, headed up the Orne River. They had a straight-in run. They would 'prang', a gliderman's term for touch-down, pointed south, along the west bank of the river, in a rectangular field nearly 1,000 metres long.

Brigadier Poett finally got his hatch open (in another of those Albemarles one of Poett's officers fell out while opening his hatch and was lost in the Channel). Standing over the hole in the floor of the bomber, a foot on each side, Poett could not see anything. He flew right over the Merville Battery, another critical target for the paras that night. Another minute and it was 0016 hours. The pilot flipped on the green light, and Poett brought his feet together and fell through the hatch into the night.

On the canal bridge, Private Romer and the other sentry were putting in another night of routine pacing back and forth across the bridge. The bombing activity up at Caen was old stuff to them, not their responsibility and not worth a glance. The men in the machine-gun pillbox dozed, as usual; so did the troops standing-to in the slit trenches. The anti-tank gun was unmanned.

In Ranville, Major Schmidt opened another bottle of wine. In Benouville, Private Bonck had finished his wine and had gone into the bedroom with his prostitute. He unbuckled his belt and began to unbutton his trousers as the woman slipped out of her dress. On the road from Ouistreham, Sergeant Hickman and his group in the staff car sped south, towards Benouville and the bridge. At the café, the Gondrées slept.

Wallwork was down to 200 feet, his airspeed slightly below 100 mph. At 0015 he was halfway down the final run. About two kilometres from his target, the clouds cleared the moon. Wallwork could see the river and the canal – they looked like strips of silver to him. Then the bridge loomed before him, exactly where he expected it. 'Well', he thought to himself, 'I gotcha now.'

CHAPTER TWO

D-Day minus two years

Spring, 1942, was a bad time for the Allies. In North Africa, the British were taking a pounding. In Russia, the Germans had launched a gigantic offensive, aimed at Stalingrad. In the Far East, the Japanese had overrun the American and British colonial possessions and were threatening Australia. In France, and throughout Western and Eastern Europe, Hitler was triumphant. The only bright spot was that America had entered the war. But to date that event had produced only a few more ships, and no troops, no planes, hardly even an increased flow of Lend-Lease supplies.

Throughout much of the British army, nevertheless, boredom reigned. The official phoney war was from September of 1939 to May of 1940, but for thousands of young men who had enlisted during that period, the time from spring, 1941 to the beginning of 1944 was almost as bad. There was no threat of invasion. The only British army doing any fighting at all was in the Mediterranean; almost everywhere else, duties and training were routine – and routinely dull. As a result, discipline had fallen off. But discipline had suffered anyway, partly because the War Office had feared to impose it too strictly in a democracy, and partly because it was thought to dampen the fighting spirit of the men in the ranks.

Obviously, many soldiers rather enjoyed this situation: they would have been more than content to stick out the war lounging around barracks, doing the odd parade or field march, otherwise finding ways of making it look as if they were busy. But there were thousands who were not content, young men who had joined up because they really did want to be soldiers,

14

really did want to fight for King and Country, really did seek some action and excitement. In the spring of 1942, their opportunity came: Britain had decided to create an airborne army under the command of Major-General F. A. M. 'Boy' Browning. This would be the 1st Airborne Division, and volunteers were being called for.

Browning had already become a legendary figure in the army. Noted especially for his tough discipline, he looked like a movie star, dressed with flair, and was married to the novelist Daphne du Maurier. It was she who in 1942 suggested a red beret for airborne troops, with Bellerophon astride winged Pegasus as the airborne shoulder patch and symbol, pale blue on a maroon background.

Wally Parr was one of the thousands who responded to the call to wear the red beret. He had joined the army in February, 1939, at the age of 16 (he was one of more than a dozen in D Company, Ox and Bucks, who lied about their age to enlist). Posted to an infantry regiment, he had spent three years 'never doing a damn thing that really mattered. Putting up barbed wire, taking it down the next day, moving it. . . . Never fired a rifle, never did a thing'. So he volunteered for airborne, passed the physical, and was accepted into the Ox and Bucks, just then forming up as an air landing unit, and assigned to D Company. After three days in his new outfit, he asked for an interview with the commander, Major John Howard.

'Ah, yes, Parr', Howard said as Parr was marched into his office. 'What can I do for you?'

'I want to get out', Parr stated. Howard stared at him. 'But you just got in.' 'Yes, sir', Parr responded, 'and I spent the last three days weeding around the barracks block. That's not what I came for. I want to transfer from here to the paras. I want the real thing, what I volunteered for, not these stupid gliders, of which we don't have any anyway.'

'Now you take it easy', Howard replied. 'Just wait.' And he dismissed Parr without another word. Leaving the office, Parr thought to himself, 'I'd better be careful with this fellow'.

In truth, Parr as yet had no idea just how tough his new company commander was. Howard was born December 8,

15

1912, eldest of nine children in a working-class London family. From the time John was two years old until he was six, his father, Jack Howard, was off in France, fighting the Great War. When Jack returned he got a job with Courage brewery, making barrels. John's mother, Ethel, a dynamic woman, managed to keep them in clean clothes and adequately fed. John recalls, 'I spent the best part of my childhood, up to the age of thirteen or fourteen, pushing prams, helping out with the shopping, and doing all that sort of thing'.

John's one great pleasure in life was the Boy Scouts. The Scouts got him out of London for weekend camps, and in the summer he would get a fortnight's camp somewhere in the country. His chums in Camden Town did not approve: they made fun of his short pants 'and generally made my life Hell'. Not even his younger brothers would stick with the Scouts. But John did. He loved the out-door life, the sports and the competition.

John's other great passion was school. He was good at his studies, especially maths, and won a scholarship to secondary school. But the financial situation at home was such that he had to go to work, so he passed up the scholarship and instead, at age fourteen, took a full-time job as a clerk with a firm of stockbrokers. He also took evening classes five nights a week in English, maths, accounting, economics, typing, shorthand, anything that he thought would be useful in his work. But in the summer of 1931, when he returned to London from Scout camp, he discovered that his firm had been hammered on the stock exchange and he was out of a job.

By this time the younger Howard children were growing, taking up more space, and the house was bursting. John offered to move out, to find a flat and a job of his own. His mother would not hear of his breaking up the family, however, so he decided to run off and enlist in the army.

He went into the King's Shropshire Light Infantry. The older soldiers, Howard found, were 'very rough and tough. . . . I freely admit I cried my eyes out for the first couple of nights when I was in the barracks room with these toughs and wondered if I'd survive.'

In fact, he began to stand out. In recruit training, at

Shrewsbury, he excelled in sports – cross-country running, swimming, boxing, all things he had done in the Scouts. To his great benefit the British army of 1932, like most peacetime regular armies everywhere, was fanatical about sports competition between platoons, companies, battalions. When John joined his battalion, at Colchester, the company commander immediately made him the company clerk, a cushy job that left him with plenty of free time for sports. Then he was sent on an education course, to learn to teach, and when he returned he was put to teaching physical education and school subjects to recruits, and to competing both for his company and battalion in various events.

That was all right, but John's ambitions reached higher. He decided to try for a commission, based on his sports record, his educational qualifications – all those night courses – and his high scores on army exams. But getting a commission from the ranks in the peacetime army was almost impossible, and he was turned down. He did get a promotion to corporal, and transferred to teach in the school at the Regimental Depot at Shrewsbury.

And he met Joy Bromley. It was a blind date, John being dragged along simply because his buddy had two girls to look after. Joy was supposed to be his buddy's date, but John took one look at her and lost his heart forever. Joy was only sixteen (she lied and told John she was seventeen), slim but with a handsome figure, pert in her face, lively in her carriage, quick to laugh, full of conversation. She had come on the date reluctantly – her people were in the retail trade in Church Stretton near Shrewsbury, she had already been dating a boy from Cambridge, and, as she told her friend, 'I'm not allowed to go out with soldiers'. 'Well, it's only for coffee', her friend persisted, 'and I've made a promise'. So Joy went, and over the coffee she and John talked, the words, the laughs, the stories bubbling out. At the train station, John kissed her good-night.

That was in 1936, and a courtship ensued. At first it was secretive, Joy fearing her mother's disapproval. They met under a large copper beech tree at the foot of the garden at Joy's house. John did not much care for this sneaking around,

17

however, and he decided to proceed on a direct line. He announced to Joy that he was going to see her mother. 'Well, I nearly died', Joy recalled. 'I thought mother wouldn't see him', and if she did, then 'she would flail me for making such an acquaintance'. But Mrs Bromley and John got along splendidly; she told Joy, 'You've got a real man there'. In April, 1937, they were engaged, promising Joy's mother they would wait until Joy was older before marrying.

In 1938, John's enlistment came to an end. In June, he joined the Oxford City Police force. After a tough, extended training course at the Police College in Birmingham, in which he came in second of 200, he began walking the streets of Oxford at night. He found it 'quite an experience. You are on your own, you know, anything can happen.'

It was here, on the streets of Oxford at midnight, with the young undergraduates staggering their way home, the occasional thief, the odd robbery, the accidents, the pub staying open after closing hour, that John Howard first came into his own. He had already demonstrated that he was reliable, exceedingly fit, a natural leader in games, a marvellous athlete himself, in short one of those you would look to for command of an infantry platoon, perhaps even a company, in time of war. But these qualities he shared with thousands of other young men. However admirable, they were hardly unique. What was unique was Howard's love of night. Not because it gave him an opportunity to indulge in some petty graft, or bash in a few heads – far from it. He loved the night because while walking his beat he had to be constantly alert.

He was a man of the most extraordinary energy, so much energy that he could not burn it off even with daily ten-mile runs and twenty miles of walking the beat. What could burn it off was the mental effort required at every corner, past every tree, literally with every step. Expecting only the unexpected, he was always on his own, with no one to turn to for reinforcements or advice. To be so intense, for such a long period of time, through the dark hours, brought Howard to a full use of all his gifts and powers. He was a creature of the night; he loved the challenge of darkness.

Howard stayed with the police until after the war began. On October 28, 1939, he and Joy were married. On December 2, he was recalled for duty as a full corporal with the 5th Battalion King's Shropshire Light Infantry, and within two weeks he was a sergeant. One month later he was Company Sergeant Major. In April, he became an Acting Regimental Sergeant Major, so he jumped from corporal to regimental sergeant major in six months, something of a record even in wartime. And in May, his Brigadier offered him a chance at a commission.

He hesitated. Being Regimental Sergeant Major meant being the top man, responsible only to the commanding officer, the real backbone of the regiment. Why give that up to be a subaltern? Further, as Howard explained to his wife, he did not have a very high opinion of the incoming second lieutenants and did not think he wanted to be a part of them. Joy brushed all his objections aside and told him that he absolutely must try for the commission. Her reaction ended his hesitance, and he went off to OCTU – Officer Cadet Training Unit – in June, 1940.

On passing out, he requested the Ox and Bucks, because he liked the association with Oxford and he liked light infantry. His first posting was to the Regimental Depot at Oxford. Within a fortnight he feared he had made a terrible mistake. The Ox and Bucks were 'a good county regiment' with a full share of battle honours, at Bunker Hill, in the Peninsula, at the Battle of New Orleans, Waterloo, and in the Great War. Half the regiment had just come back from India. All the officers came from the upper classes. It was in the nature of things for them to be snobbish, especially to a working-class man who had been a cop and had come up from the ranks. In brief, the officers cut Howard. They meant it to be sharp and cruel, and it was, and it hurt.

After two weeks of the silent treatment, Howard phoned Joy, then living with her family in Shropshire. 'You'd better plan to move here', he told her. 'Because it's just horrible and I need some encouragement or I am not going to stick it. I don't have to put up with this.' Joy promised him she would move quickly.

The following morning, on the parade ground, Howard was putting four squads through different kinds of training. He already had his men sharp enough to do some complicated manoeuvres. When he dismissed the squads, he turned to see his colonel standing behind him. In a quiet voice, the colonel asked, 'Why don't you bring your wife here, Howard?' It was a sure indication that the C.O. wanted to keep him in Oxford and not follow the normal routine of being posted to a Battalion. Within a week, they had found a flat in Oxford and John had been accepted by his fellow officers.

Soon he was a captain with his own company, which he trained for the next year. At the beginning of 1942, he learned that a decision had been taken for the 2nd Battalion of the Ox and Bucks to go airborne in gliders. No one was forced to go airborne; every officer and trooper was given a choice. About 30 per cent declined the opportunity to wear the red beret, and another 20 per cent were weeded out in the physical exam. It was meant to be an elite regiment. The sergeant major came to the Ox and Bucks specially posted from the outside, and he was everything a regimental sergeant major from the Guards' Honour Regiment should be. Wally Parr speaks of the man's overpowering personality: 'That first day', says Parr, 'he called the whole bleeding company together on parade. And he looked at us, and we looked at him, and we both knew who was boss.'

Howard himself had to give up his company and his captaincy to go airborne, but he did not hesitate. He reverted to lieutenant and platoon leader in order to become an airborne officer. In three weeks, his colonel promoted him and gave him command of D Company. Shortly after that, in May of 1942, he was promoted to major.

The men of D Company – half from the original Ox and Bucks, half from volunteers drawn from every branch of the army – came from all over the United Kingdom, and from every class and occupation. What they had in common was that they were young, fit, eager to be trained, ready for excitement. They were the kind of troops every company commander wishes he could have.

Howard's platoon leaders also came from different back-grounds. Two were Cambridge students when they volun-teered, and one was a graduate of the University of Bristol. But the oldest lieutenant, at age twenty-six, was Den Brotheridge, who, like Howard, had come up from the ranks. Indeed, Howard had originally recommended Den, then a corporal at the Regimental Depot, for OCTU. His fellow platoon leaders were a bit uneasy about Den when he first joined up; as one of them explained, 'He wasn't one of us, you know'. Den played football rather than rugby. But, the officer immediately added, 'You couldn't help but like him'. Den was a first-class athlete, good enough that it was freely predicted he would become a professional football player after the war.

Captain Brian Priday was Howard's second-in-command. Six feet tall, a quiet steady type, Priday was ideal for the job. He and Howard hit it off, helped by the fact that Priday's father had also been in the Oxford Police force. Priday himself had been in the motor car trade. He was in his mid-twenties. Lieutenants Tod Sweeney and Tony Hooper were in their early twenties; Lieutenant David Wood was all of nineteen years old, fresh out of OCTU. 'My gracious', Howard thought to himself when Wood reported, 'he is going to be a bit too young for the toughies in my company'. But, Howard added, 'David was so clean and bubbling with enthusiasm I thought, "well, we've got to make something of him". So I gave him a young soldier platoon with mature NCOs.'

Sweeney describes himself and his fellow subalterns as 'irresponsible young men. Life was very light-hearted, there was a war on, lots of fun for us. John was a dedicated and serious trainer and we were rather like young puppies he was trying to train.'

Brotheridge provided enthusiasm and humour for the group. He would gather the platoon leaders together, then read to them from Jerome K. Jerome's *Three Men in a Boat*. They could scarcely get through a sentence without breaking down in peals of laughter. Weekend evenings they would drop into the lobby of the local hotel, where a good number of 'dear old ladies from London, who wanted to escape the bombing, had taken up residence for the duration'. Den and his cohorts would sit properly enough, but then Den would start whispering orders. The grandfather clock was the objective – David was to sneak behind the sofa, climb over the bar, go through the kitchen, and attack the clock from the rear; Tod should leap out the window,

21

dash around to the door, and charge in to attack from the side – and so on. Then Den would shout, 'Go', and the ladies watched aghast as these young men dashed about.

Howard was pleased with his company, officers and men. He especially liked having so many Londoners in it. The regiment moved to Bulford, where D Company was given a spider block, near the barracks but separate from it. So, Howard notes, 'right from the first there was an atmosphere of D Company being on its own'. He set out to make it into both a family and a first-class combat unit.

In North Africa, Hans von Luck was fighting in the only war he ever enjoyed. As commander of the armed reconnaissance battalion on Rommel's extreme right (southern) flank, he enjoyed a certain independence, and so did his British opposite number. The two commanding officers agreed to fight a civilised war. Every day at 5 p.m. the war shut down, the British to brew up their tea, the Germans their coffee. At about 5:15, von Luck and the British commander would communicate over the radio. 'Well', von Luck might say, 'we captured so-and-so today, and he's fine, and he sends his love to his mother, tell her not to worry'. Once von Luck learned that the British had received a month's supply of cigarettes. He offered to trade a captured officer for one million cigarettes. The British countered with an offer of 600,000. Done, said von Luck. But the British prisoner was outraged. He said the ransom was insufficient. He insisted he was worth the million and refused to be exchanged.

One evening, an excited corporal reported that he had just stolen a British truck, jammed with tinned meat and other delicacies. Von Luck looked at his watch – it was past 6 p.m. – and told the corporal he would have to take it back, as he had captured it after 5. The corporal protested that this was war and anyway the troops were already gathering in the goods from the truck. Von Luck called Rommel, his mentor in military academy. He said he was suspicious of British moves further south and thought he ought to go out on a two-day reconnaissance. Could another battalion take his place for that time? Rommel agreed. The new battalion arrived in the morning.

That night, at 5:30 p.m., just as von Luck had anticipated, the British stole *two* supply trucks.

Heinrich Hickman, meanwhile, had gone through the campaigns in Holland, Belgium and France of 1940 as a gunner on an 88mm gun. In 1941, he volunteered for the parachute regiment, and went to Spandau for jump school. In May, 1942, he was in the middle of his training.

In Warsaw, Vern Bonck was doing his best to stay out of the German conscription net by working with extra efficiency at his lathe. Helmut Romer, fourteen years old, was finishing his school year in Berlin.

At the bridge over the Caen canal, there were as yet no elaborate defences, and only a tiny garrison. Still, the garrison was large enough to make the lives of the people of Benouville, Le Port, and Ranville miserable. The Germans helped themselves to the best of everything, paid for what they did purchase with nearly worthless printing-press francs, took all the young men away for slave labour, made travel even within the country almost impossible, imposed a curfew, and shot dissenters. By May, 1942, the Gondrées had decided to do something about it. Georges joined the local Resistance, which advised him to stay put and use his situation to gather information on the bridges and their defence. This he could easily do on the basis of what his wife heard in the café. Let there be no mistake about this action – the Gondrées knew that if the Germans caught them, they would be first tortured, then hanged. But they persisted.

In May, 1942, Jim Wallwork was also in training camp. Jim was a Manchester lad who had volunteered for the army at age 19, in 1939. His father, who had been an artilleryman in the Great War, had advised him, 'Whatever you do, Jim, don't for God's sake join the infantry. Get in the artillery, the biggest gun you can find; if possible, the railway gun.' Naturally, Jim ended up in the infantry, bored to tears, although he did make it to sergeant. He tried to transfer out, into the Royal Air Force, but his commanding officer blocked the move because he wanted to keep Wallwork with him.

Then in early 1942, when a call went out for volunteers for

the Glider Pilots Regiment, Jim signed up. By spring he was training at Tilshead, Salisbury Plain. 'It was rather rough', he recalled, 'because I was doing my own equipment, polishing my own brass, going on those God-awful run-marches, and drills, and all sorts of that nonsense.' What he most feared, what every man in the Glider Pilots Regiment most feared, were the letters, 'RTU'. They stood for Return to Unit, and they meant disgrace, failure. Jim managed to stick it, and by May, 1942, he was at flight training school, learning to fly a small aeroplane.

Howard's own family was growing. Joy, living with relatives at Church Stretton, was pregnant. During the war Howard was a virtual teetotaller, partly because he wanted to keep a clear mind, partly because 'I saw the mess a lot of people were getting into, making bloody fools of themselves, and I wanted to set an example for my own subalterns'. The child was due in late June but not actually born until July 12. During the fortnight between the due date and the actual delivery, Howard was so irritable and bad-tempered that his subalterns found him unapproachable. When news of the successful delivery arrived in Bulford, everyone was so relieved that a huge party developed. Howard, drinking straight shots of whisky 'to wet the baby's head', got royally drunk.

By July, Howard was pretty much on his own, allowed by his colonel to set his own training pace and schedule. Initially he put the emphasis on teaching the men the skills of the light infantryman. He taught them to be marksmen with their rifles, with the light machine-gun, with the carbine and the pistol, with the Piat and other anti-tank weapons. He instructed them in the many types of grenades, their characteristics and special uses.

The basic weapons of a gliderborne platoon of thirty men included the Enfield .303 rifle, the Sten carbine, the Bren light machine gun, 2″ and 3″ mortars, and the Piat (projector infantry anti-tank). The Enfield was the old reliable British rifle. One or two men in each platoon were snipers, each equipped with a telescopic sight for his rifle. The Sten was a 9mm submachine gun that reflected Britain's inability to produce quality weapons for her troops. The Sten was mass-produced, and distributed to thousands of fighting men, not because it was good but because it was cheap. It could be fired single-shot or automatic, but the weapon frequently jammed and too often it went off on its own. In 1942 David Wood accidentally shot Den Brotheridge in the leg with his Sten, in fact, after forgetting to put the safety-catch back on. Brotheridge recovered, and indeed he, like all the officers, carried the Sten by choice. Weighing only seven pounds and measuring thirty inches in length, it had an effective range of a hundred yards and used a box magazine holding thirty-two rounds. For all its shortcomings, it was deadly in close-in combat – if it worked.

The Bren gun was a light machine gun, weighing twenty-three pounds, normally fired on the ground from a tripod, but also from the hip. It had an effective range of 500 yards and a rate of fire of 120 rounds per minute. There was one Bren gunner per platoon; everyone in the platoon helped carry the thirty-round magazines for him. In rate of fire, in depend ability, and by other measurements, the Bren was inferior to its German counterpart, the MG 34, just as the Sten was inferior to the German Schmeisser.

The Piat was a hand-held rocket, fired from the shoulder, that threw a three-pound bomb through a barrel at high trajectory and a speed of about 300 feet per second. The hollow charged bomb exploded on impact. Effective range was supposed to be 100 yards, but the men of D Company could never get more than 50 yards out of the Piat. Being spring-loaded, Piats were inaccurate and subject to frequent jamming. They also had a nasty habit of glancing off the target unexploded. No one liked them very much, but all got proficient with them.

They all also learned to use a Gammon bomb, a plastic explosive charge developed from the 'Sticky Bomb' and designed by Captain Gammon of the paratroopers. You could throw one with a stick and it would cling to the clogs of a tank, or even throw it by hand (as long as it did not stick to the hand). Except for the Piat, Gammon bombs were all a glider platoon had to fight tanks, and the men learned what they had to know about them. Much of the training was with live ammunition, which caused some accidents and an occasional death, but the British had learned from Dieppe that it was essential to expose green troops to live ammunition before sending them into combat.

Howard taught his men about German weapons, how to use them, what they could do. He taught them how to lay and find mines, how to take them up. He gave them a working knowledge of elementary first aid, of cooking in a billy can, of the importance of keeping clean. He made certain that they could recognise the smell of various poison gases, and knew what to do if attacked by them. He insisted that every man in his company be proficient in the use of natural and artificial camouflage, and know how to read a topographical map. His men had to know how to use a field wireless, how to drive various army vehicles. Most of all, Howard put the emphasis on teaching them to think quickly. They were elite, he told them, they were glider-borne troops, and wherever and whenever it was that they attacked the enemy, they could be sure of the need for quick thinking and quick response.

Howard's emphasis on technical training went a bit beyond what the other company commanders were doing, but only just a bit. Each of Howard's associates were commanding top-quality volunteers, and were volunteers themselves, outstanding officers. What was different about D Company was its commander's mania for physical fitness. It went beyond anything anyone in the regiment had ever seen before. All the regiment prided itself on being fit (one officer from B Company described himself as a physical-fitness fanatic), but all were amazed, and a bit critical, of the way Howard pushed his company fitness programme.

D Company's day began with a five-mile cross-country run, done at a speed of seven or eight minutes to the mile. After that the men dressed, ate breakfast, and then spent the day on training exercises, usually strenuous. In the late afternoon, Howard insisted that everyone engage in some sport or another. His own favourites were the individual endeavours, cross-country running, swimming, and boxing, but he encouraged football, rugby, and any sport that would keep his lads active until bedtime.

Those were regular days. Twice a month, Howard would take the whole company out for two or three days, doing field exercises, sleeping rough. He put them through gruelling marches and soon they became an outstanding marching unit. Wally Parr swears – and a number of his comrades back him up – that they could do twenty-two miles, in full pack, including the Brens, mortars and ammunition, in under five and one-half hours. When they got back from such a march, Parr relates, 'you would have a foot inspection, get a bite to eat, and then in the afternoon face a choice: either play football or go for a cross-country run'.

All the officers, including Howard, did everything the men did. All of them had been athletes themselves, and loved sports and competition. The sports and the shared misery on the forced marches were bringing officers and men closer together. David Wood was exceedingly popular with his platoon, as was Tod Sweeney, in his own quiet way, with his. But Brotheridge stood out. He played the men's game, football, and as a former corporal himself he had no sense of being ill at ease among the men. He would come into their barracks at night, sit on the bed of his batman, Billy Gray, and talk football with the lads. He got to bringing his boots along, and shining them as he talked. Wally Parr never got over the sight of a British lieutenant polishing his boots himself while his batman lay back on his bed, gassing on about Manchester United and West Ham and other football teams.

Howard's biggest problem was boredom. He wracked his brains to find different ways of doing the same things, to put some spontaneity into the training. His young heroes had many virtues, but patience was not one of them. The resulting morale problem extended far beyond D Company, obviously, and late in the summer of 1942, General Gale sent the whole regiment to Devonshire for two months of cliff climbing, and other strenuous training. He then decided to march the regiment back to Bulford, some 130 miles. Naturally, it would be a competition between the companies.

The first two days were the hottest of the summer, and the men were marching in serge, ringing with sweat. After the second day, they pleaded for permission to change to lighter gear. It was granted, and over the next two days a cold, hard rain beat down on their inadequately-covered bodies.

Howard marched up and down the column, urging his men on. He had a walking stick, an old army one with an inch of brass on the bottom. His company clerk and wireless operator, Corporal Tappenden, offered the major the use of his bike. He refused, growling. 'I'm leading my company'. From gripping the stick his hands grew more blisters than Tappenden's feet, and he wore away all the brass on the end of it. But he kept marching.

On the morning of the fourth day, when Howard roused the men and ordered them to fall in, Wally Parr and his friend Jack Bailey waddled out on their knees. When Howard asked them what they thought they were doing, Wally replied that he and Jack had worn away the bottom half of their legs. But they got up and marched. 'Mad bastard', the men whispered among themselves after Howard had moved off. 'Mad, ambitious bastard. He'll get us all killed.' But they marched.

D Company got back to base on the evening of the fifth day, marching in at 145 steps to the minute and singing 'Onward Christian Soldiers'. Loudly. They came in first in the regiment, by half a day. Howard had lost only two men out of 120. (His stick, however, became so worn that he had to throw it away.)

Howard had radioed ahead, and had hot showers and meals waiting for the men. As the officers began to undress for their showers, Howard told them to button up. They had to go do a foot inspection of the men, then watch to make sure they all showered properly, check on the quality and quantity of their food, and inspect the barracks to see that the beds were ready. By the time the officers got to shower, the hot water was gone; by the time they got to eat, only cold leftovers remained. But not a one of them had let Howard down.

'From then on', Howard recalls, 'we didn't follow the normal pattern of training.' His colonel gave him even more flexibility, and the transport to make it meaningful. Howard started taking his company to Southampton, or London, or Portsmouth, to conduct street fighting exercises in the bombed-out areas. There were plenty to choose from, and it did not matter how much damage D Company did, so all the exercises were with live ammunition.

Howard was putting together an oustanding light infantry company.

CHAPTER THREE

D-Day minus one year to D-Day minus one month

By the spring of 1943, the British airborne force had become large enough to be divided into two divisions. The 1st Airborne went off to North Africa while the 6th (the number was chosen to confuse German intelligence) was formed around the units that stayed behind, including the Ox and Bucks and D Company.

General Richard Gale, known to everyone as 'Windy' because of his last name, commanded 6th Airborne Division. A large, confident, experienced officer who had commanded the 1st Para Brigade, Gale had a bit of the buccaneer about him, and more than a bit of imagination to complement his professionalism.

Nigel Poett commanded the 5th Para Brigade. He was a regular officer from the Durham Light Infantry. A big, powerful man, Poett was meticulous on detail and an officer who led from the front. The 3rd Para Brigade was commanded by James Hill, a regular from the Royal Fusiliers who had won a DSO in North Africa. D Company was a part of the Airlanding Brigade, commanded by Brigadier Hugh Kindersley.*

Training intensified under Gale's prodding, but there were few complaints because the word was that the division was being prepared for the invasion of France. Gale, through his training exercises, was trying to figure out what the division was capable of performing, while simultaneously trying to figure out exactly how he would use it to achieve his D-Day objectives.

*After the war Kindersley became chairman of Rolls-Royce and was made a peer.

At COSSAC (Chief of Staff, Supreme Allied Command), planning for Gale's role, and for the invasion as a whole, had been going on for a year, under the direction of General Frederick Morgan. By the spring of 1943, Morgan and his planners had settled on Normandy, west of the mouth of the Orne River, as the invasion site. A variety of factors influenced the choice; the one that affected D Company and the 6th Airborne Division was the need to protect the left flank of the seaborne invasion, where the British 3rd Division would be landing on Sword Beach. That left flank was the single most vulnerable point in the whole invasion, because to the east, beyond Le Havre and the mouth of the Seine River, the Germans had the bulk of their armour in the West. If Rommel brought that armour across the Seine, crossed the River Dives and the Orne River, then launched an all-out counter-attack against the exposed flank of 3rd Division, he might well roll up the entire invading force, division by division. It would take days for the Allies to unload enough tanks and artillery of their own to withstand such a blow.

Morgan and his people decided to meet the threat by placing the 6th Airborne between the Orne waterways and the River Dives. There were many changes in the COSSAC plan after January, 1944, when Eisenhower took over SHAEF (Supreme Headquarters, Allied Expeditionary Force) and Montgomery took over at 21st Army Group, which commanded all the ground forces; the most important change was the widening of the assault area from three to five divisions. But one COSSAC decision that remained unchanged was the one that placed 6th Airborne on its own, east of the Orne River, with the task of holding off armoured counter-attacks. How to do it was left to General Gale.

D Company had begun its flight training in little Waco gliders. To begin with Howard concentrated on exit drill. The door was open before the glider touched down and it was 'move, move, move' when the glider hit the ground. Again and again Howard reminded the men that they were 'rats-in-a-trap' so long as they were inside.

The chief novelty of flying in a glider was one Howard could

TOPOGRAPHICAL REPORT ON BRIDGES AT BENOUVILLE 098748 AND RANVILLE 104746

1. Sketch - BENOUVILLE 098748

Control
Mechanism

10'-15' high
embankment

2. Description of canal and immediate vicinity

   (a) The current is slow. Depth reported to be 27' but can be regulated by
       the locks at OUISTREHAM. Average width 150'. Banks average 6' in
       height, and are of earth and broken stone.

   (b) A track with waterbound macadam surface runs for most of the length of
       the canal on both sides.
       On the WEST bank there is a lt rly (single track).
       Either bank of the canal is lined with poplars.
       On each side of the br there are a few small houses. (For detail see
       large scale model).

   (c) The rd leading up to the br is on a 10'-15' high embankment to keep it
       above the flood level.

3. Description of Br

   (a) The water gap is 190' but from either bank there are abutments which
       project 50' into the stream.

   (b) The br is a steel girder, rolling lift br with masonry abutments.
       Control mechanism is located in a cabin over rdway.
       Overall length of br 190'
       Lifting span 90'
       Rd width 12', rdway ashphalt or steel.

   (c) The br is reported as being mined. (Prepared for demolition).

4. Defs of Canal

   (a) WEST bank open MG emplacements are visible on the canal banks on each
       side of the br approach.
       There are further open MG emplacements at 098748(2), 097748(2) and
       096746.

   (b) EAST side. SOUTH of rd close to the canal bank is a circular emplace-
       ment approx 27' in diameter which is probable site for an tk gun but
       the object in the emplacement cannot be identified as a gun.
       25 yds SOUTH of the above is an AA MG post on a tower 8' high.

   (c) 60 yds NORTH of the rd close to the canal are 3 open MG emplacements,
       12 yds apart, in a line facing NE.
       Approx 16 yds NE of these emplacements is a concrete shelter or pill-
       box, measuring approx 17' x 14'.
   (d) No wire defs are visible.

   (e) Armed trawlers and R Boats may be used in canal but this is considered
       unlikely.

........../5..........

5. **Description of R ORNE**

   (a) Average width 160' – 240'.
   Tidal as far as CAEN.
   Mean depth 9'
   Max tidal variation at OUISTREHAM 16'.
       "   "   "   " CAEN 6'5".
   Banks 3'6" high, of mud, and slope at approx 1 : 2.

   (b) There is a barrage at CAEN which regulates the canal at the expense
   of the river, hence speed and depth will vary considerably. Max
   current will probably NOT exceed 3 Knots.

   (c) Ground between the river and canal is marshy and intersected by many
   ditches and channels.

   (d) A track 8'-10' wide runs on both sides of the river for most of its
   length.

6. **Description of br 104745 and immediate vicinity.**

   (a) The br is a two span, cantilever lattice girder, pivoted about a
   central masonry pier. Turning mechanism is housed over pier between
   girders.
   Overall length of br 350'.
   Spans, 2 at 100'.
   Load class 12.
   Rdway – 9' tarmac (20' incl sidewalks).
   It is thought that this br may no longer be used as a swing br.
   Br has been reported as prepared for demolition.

   (b) SOUTH of the rd and WEST of the river is an orchard running NORTH
   and SOUTH.
   Each bank of the river is lined with poplars.
   On the EAST of the river and SOUTH of the rd is a thick belt of
   trees running parallel to the river, and about 50 yds away.
   Both NORTH and SOUTH of the rd there are a few small houses,
   standing in gardens or orchards. For details see large scale model.

7. **Defs on R ORNE**

   (a) <u>EAST end</u> and on the SOUTH side of the rd is a cam pill-box measuring
   approx 16' x 16'. This may contain an a tk weapon with main line
   of fire EAST along rd.
   There is a small AAMG emplacement adjoining this pill-box on the
   WEST side.

   (b) <u>EAST side.</u> Two open MG emplacements are visible on the NORTH side
   of the rd.
   (c) There is no wire visible.
   (d) Two rd-blocks (probably tree trunks) lie alongside the rd at 105745
   and 106744.

   BQ Gillow Capt
   T Maj
   Br 6 Airldg Bde

1 Topographical report on the bridges dated 17 May 1944. The superb quality of the
information provided by both the French Resistance and reconnaissance aircraft is
apparent.

not get over. As General Sir Napier Crookenden wrote in *Dropzone Normandy*: 'Since the glider on the end of its tug-rope moved in a series of surges as the tug-rope tightened and slackened, and was subject to the normal pitching, rolling and yawing of any aircraft, few men survived more than half an hour without being sick. The floor was soon awash with vomit, and this in itself was enough to defeat the strongest stomach.' Howard could not get away from being sick; he threw up on all twelve of his training flights. Fortunately for him, this was not like being seasick, with its long recovery time. After being sick on a glider flight, Howard was fit and ready as soon as his feet hit the ground.

Howard's sickness gave the men a great laugh, something the company badly needed as it was in danger of going stale. Wally Parr described morale in late 1943, when the Yanks began appearing:

'Then in came the big spending Americans at Tidworth and the fights that used to take place in Salisbury was nobody's business, 'cause from Tidworth you had to go through Bulford by transport to get to Salisbury, and they were stationed, thousands of them, mountains of planes at Tidworth there and there was sheer frustration all the time, you know, and it was nothing unusual to go in Saturday night, you've got a couple of bob in your pocket, a couple of beers and then, of course, the fights usually started. In the majority of cases the birds went with the Yanks, 'cause the Yanks had more money and could show them a good time.'

In barracks, there were worse fights, as Parr relates:

'We would be sleeping, midnight, and all of a sudden the door burst open and in would come a load of screaming maniacs from Sweeney's platoon, throw the beds up in the air, the whole lot. I'm talking about "thunder-flashes" that we used to use for exercises and that, just throwing them about the place, left, right, smoke stuff, a lot of it. It was sheer vitality coupled with total frustration.'

Parr, by this time a corporal in charge of the snipers, could not stand the boredom any longer.

'Me and Billy Gray and another fellow was bored one night so we decided, just for the fun of it, we'd go and rob the NAAFI so we waited until it was pretty dark and then we drifted off to sleep and forgot it, then we woke up about five o'clock and thought, ah, Hell, we might as well, so we went over and we broke into the NAAFI and we emptied it of soap, soap powder and everything and came back with it in sackfuls which we spread all over the cobblestones and pavement. A nice rain stirred it up. You've never seen so much soap in all your life. It was bonjour soap, personnel, oxydyl, everything was foam.'

Howard busted Wally back to private and sentenced him to a fortnight in jail; he put Billy Gray and the other man in the jail for twenty-eight days. Howard's colonel, Mike Roberts, wanted to RTU Private Parr, but Howard protested that the punishment was excessive, and in any case told Roberts, 'Parr might only be a private but he is the man that when I get to the other side he will be promoted straightaway, he is a born leader.' Roberts let Howard keep Parr. There were a number of similar cases; Howard called them 'my scalawags' and says, 'when we got to the other side, they were the best. In battle they were in their natural environment. Unfortunately, most of them were killed because of their nature and their way of going about things.' He did re-promote Parr on D-Day plus two.

Howard's solution for boredom was to keep the men physically exhausted, and he drove himself hardest of all. He would go for long periods with only two or three hours of sleep per day, preparing himself for what he anticipated would be a major problem in combat – making quick decisions with an exhausted mind.

Howard also set out, on his own, to make D Company into a first-class night-fighting unit. It was not that he had any inkling that he might be landing at night, but rather that he reckoned that once in combat, his troops would be spending a good deal of their time fighting at night. He was also thinking of an expression he had heard was used in the German army: 'The night is the friend of no man.' In the British army, the saying was that 'the German does not like to fight at night'.

35

The trouble was, neither did the British. (Nor did the Canadians, Americans, or French for that matter.) The Russians and Chinese seemed to be best in this night-fighting business, possibly because while Western men were afraid of the dark, having lived all their lives with electricity, Eastern men were accustomed to it. Howard decided to deal with the problem of fighting in unaccustomed darkness by turning night into day. He would rouse the company at 2000 hours, take the men for their run, get them fed, and then begin twelve hours of field exercises, drill, the regular paperwork – everything that a company in training does in the course of a day. After a meal at 1000 hours, he would get them going on the athletic fields. At 1300 hours he sent them to barracks. At 2000 hours, they were up again, running. This would go on for a week at a time at first; by early 1944, said Parr, 'we went several weeks, continuous weeks of night into day and every now and then he would have a change-around week'. And they gradually became accustomed to operating in the dark of night.

None of the other companies in the division were doing night into day anything like so consistently, and this added to D Company's feeling of independence and separateness. All the sports fanaticism had produced, as Howard hoped that it would, an extreme competitiveness. The men wanted D Company to be first, in everything, and they had indeed won the regimental prizes in boxing, swimming, cross-country, football, and other sports. When Brigadier Kindersley asked to observe a race among the best runners in the division, D Company had entered twenty runners and took fifteen of the first twenty places. According to Howard, Kindersley 'was just cock-a-hoop about it'.

That was exactly the response for which Howard and his company had been working so hard. The ultimate competitiveness would come against the Germans, of course, but next best was competing against the other companies. D Company wanted to be first among all the glider-borne companies, not just for the thrill of victory, but because victory in this contest meant a unique opportunity to be a part of history. No one could guess what it might be, but even the lowest private could figure out that the War Office was not going to spend all that money building an elite force and then not use it in the invasion. It was equally obvious that airborne troops would be among the first to engage in combat, almost certainly behind enemy lines – thus an heroic adventure of unimaginable dimensions. And, finally, it was obvious that the best company would play a leading role in the fighting. That was the thought that sustained Howard and his company through the long dreary months, now stretching into two years, of training. The thought sustained them because, whether consciously or subconsciously, to a man they were aware that D-Day would be the greatest day of their lives. Neither what had happened before, nor what would come after, could possibly compare. D Company continued to work at a pace that bordered on fanaticism in order to earn the right to be the first to go.

By spring, 1943, Jim Wallwork had completed his glider pilot training, most of it using Hotspurs; in the process he survived a gruelling course that less than one-third of the volunteers passed. After passing out, Wallwork and his twenty-nine fellow pilots went to Brize Norton, an old peacetime aerodrome, 'and that is where we saw our first wheel glider which was the Horsa, and we immediately fell in love with it'.

The Horsa was a product of Britain's total war effort. In 1940, the Air Ministry, responding to the need to conserve critical metals and the need to draw the wood-working industries into war-time production, ordered an all-wooden glider. The prototypes were built at what is now Heathrow Airport; five more were built at Airspeed's Portsmouth works, which went on to build 700 production models. The Horsa must have been the most wooden aircraft ever built; even the controls in the cockpit were masterpieces of the woodworker's artistry. A high-wing monoplane with a large plexiglass nose and a tricycle landing gear, it had a wing span of eighty-eight feet and a fuselage length of sixty-seven feet. It could carry a pilot and a co-pilot, plus 28 fully-armed men, or two jeeps, or a 75mm howitzer, or a quarter-ton truck.

The pilots were immensely impressed by the Horsa, especially by its size. 'It was like a big, black crow', said Wallwork. 'But when we first got in before we ever flew and felt the controls, saw the size of the flaps, we were very impressed, particularly so since we were going to have to fly it.' The seats in the cockpit were side-by-side and very big; visibility through the front and side was excellent. Each pilot had proper dual controls, and the instruments included an air-speed indicator, a turn and bank indicator, air pressure gauge, compass, and altimeter.

'Flying a glider', according to Wallwork, 'is just like flying an aircraft. The instruments and controls are the same; the only thing that is short in the glider is the rev counter and the temperature gauge. Really, flying a glider on tow is just the same as flying an aircraft except that the engine is 100 yards ahead and someone else is in control of the engine.'

The glider was tugged on a rope with a Y arrangement; there was a line on each wing that came together in front of the nose and ran on as a single line to the bomber doing the tugging. A telephone line ran along the rope, making it possible for the pilot of the bomber and the glider pilot to communicate.

By mid-spring, Wallwork had qualified on Horsas, one of the first to do so. He was then shipped down to North Africa.

In March, 1943, Rommel called von Luck to come see him at his headquarters near Benghazi. Von Luck drove up and together they dealt with some of the supply problems. Then Rommel asked von Luck to go for a walk. Rommel regarded von Luck almost as a second son, and he wanted to talk. 'Listen', Rommel said. 'One day you will remember what I am telling you. The war is lost.'

Von Luck protested. 'We are very deep in Russia', he exclaimed. 'We are in Scandinavia, in France, in the Balkans, in North Africa. How can the war be lost?'

'I will tell you', Rommel answered. 'We lost Stalingrad, we will lose Africa, with the body of our best trained armoured people. We can't fight without them. The only thing we can do is to ask for an armistice. We have to give up all this business about the Jews, we have to change our minds about the religions, and so on, and we must get an armistice now at this stage while we still have something to offer.'

Rommel asked von Luck to fly to Hitler's headquarters and plead with the Führer to execute a Dunkirk in reverse. It was all up in North Africa for the Axis, Rommel said, and he wanted to save his Afrika Korps. Von Luck went, but did not get past Field Marshal Jodl, who told von Luck that the Führer was in political discussions with the Rumanians and nobody wanted to butt in with military decisions, 'and anyway', Jodl concluded, 'there's no idea at all to withdraw from North Africa'. Von Luck never returned to Tunisia. Rommel flew out. The Afrika Korps was destroyed or captured.

Von Luck went on to teach at the military academy for six months. Late in the autumn of 1943 he got orders to join the 21st Panzer Division in Brittany as one of the two regimental commanders. He had been specially requested by the division commander, Brigadier-General Edgar Feuchtinger, who was close to Hitler and thus got the officers he wanted. Feuchtinger was reviving 21st Panzer from the dead, but his contact with Hitler made it a feasible task. His officers were exclusively veterans and the troops – almost 16,000 of them, as this was a full-strength division – were volunteers, young, eager, fit. The equipment was excellent, especially the tanks. In addition, the new 21st Panzer had an abundance of SPVs (self-propelled vehicles), put together by a Major Becker, a genius with transport who could transform any type of chassis into a SPV. On his SPVs he would mount all sorts of guns, but his favourite was the so-called Stalin organ, or rocket launcher with forty-eight barrels.

Von Luck set to with his regiment, giving the men extended night-training drills among other exercises. When Rommel took command of the German 7th Army in Normandy and Brittany, he injected badly needed enthusiasm and professional skill into the building of the Atlantic Wall.

Even Major Schmidt, guarding the bridges over the Orne waterways, caught some of the enthusiasm. He had come to Normandy some months earlier and quickly adjusted from frantic Nazi to a garrison soldier ready to enjoy the slow pace of the Norman countryside. He had put his men to work digging bunkers and slit trenches, and even an open machine-gun pit; with Rommel's arrival, the pace of construction speeded up, and the scope of the defensive emplacements was greatly increased.

In March, 1944, two reinforcements arrived at the bridge. One was Vern Bonck, who had got caught by the Gestapo in Warsaw, sent to a six-week training camp, where he could hardly understand the German NCOs, and then posted to the 716th Infantry Division on the coast north of Caen. Helmut Romer had finished his Berlin schooling, been drafted, sent to training camp, and then also posted to the 716th.

Heinrich Hickman spent most of 1943 fighting. He got out of North Africa just in time, participated in the campaign in Sicily, then fought at Salerno and Cassino. At Cassino his regiment took such heavy losses that it had to be pulled back to Bologna for rebuilding and training recruits. Through the winter of 1943–4, Hickman and his parachute regiment, like Howard and D Company, like von Luck and 21st Panzer, were training, training, training.

In June, 1943, Jim Wallwork went to Algeria, where he learned to fly the Waco glider, an American-built craft that landed on skids. These carried only thirteen men, were difficult to handle, and were altogether despised by the British Glider Pilots Regiment. The pilots were delighted when they heard that Oliver Boland and some others were going to fly a few Horsas down to North Africa, all the way from England. Wallwork told his American instructors, 'You, you be here tomorrow, you've got to be here to see a proper bloody glider. You'll really see something'. Then, 'by golly, here came the first Halifax and Horsa combination'. Turning to his instructor, Wallwork bellowed, 'Look at that, you bloody Yank, there's a proper aeroplane, a proper glider, that's a proper thing. Oh, the truth of it!'

The Horsa cast off, did a circuit, came down, 'and broke its bloody nose off. Imagine this. It was the first one in. Well, our American friends were delighted about that.'

On the day of the invasion of Sicily, Jim flew a Waco with a lieutenant, ten riflemen, and a hand-trailer full of ammunition. The tug pilots were Americans, flying Dakotas, which had no self-sealing tanks and no armoured plate. Their orders were to avoid flak at all costs. When they approached the coast line and flak began to appear, most of the American pilots cast off their gliders and turned back to sea. As a consequence of being let go too far out, twenty of the twenty-four gliders never made it to shore. Many of the men were drowned, and upon hearing this news, John Howard stepped up his swimming requirements.

In Jim's case, he kept telling the Dakota pilot, 'Get in, get in'. But instead the pilot turned away to sea, made a second run, and told Jim to drop off. Jim refused, seeing that the coast was too far away, and he again yelled, 'Get in, get in'. A third try, a third refusal by Jim to be let go. On the fourth pass, the Dakota pilot said calmly but firmly, 'James, I'm going now. You've got to let go.' Jim let go thinking he could just make it. He did, skidding in just over the beach, on a little rough field, fairly close to an Italian machine-gun nest. The Italians opened fire, 'and we all jumped out; we knew by then to get out of the glider quickly'. Jim turned his Sten gun on the Italians, thinking to himself, 'Right, this will do you buggers'. He pulled the trigger and nothing happened. The Sten had misfired. But the Bren gun knocked out the opposition. As the section then began to unload the glider, the lieutenant asked Wallwork, 'Well, where in the Hell are we? Do you know where we are?'

'As a matter of fact, sir', Jim replied, 'I think you should be congratulated. I think you are the first Allied officer to attack the soft underbelly of Europe through the toe of Italy.' Wallwork claims today that he was so confused by all the passes he had made at the beach that he really did think he had come down on the Continent proper. Later that autumn, he was shipped back to England, to participate in operation Deadstick.

Deadstick was the result of decisions General Gale had made. Studying his tactical problem, he had decided that the best way to provide protection for the left flank of Sword Beach would be to blow up the bridges over the River Dives, through paratrooper assaults, then gather his paras some five miles or so west of Dives, in a semi-circle around the waterway bridges at Ranville and Benouville. Without those bridges, the Germans could not get at the left flank of the invasion. Gale could not afford to simply blow up the Orne bridges, however, because without them he would have an entire airborne division in the middle of enemy territory, its back to a major water barrier, without proper anti-tank weapons or other crucial supplies, and with no means of getting them.

The bridges had to be taken intact. Gale knew that they had a garrison guarding them, and that they had been prepared for demolition. Paras might be able to take the bridges, and could certainly destroy them, but would probably not be able to capture them intact. The relative slowness with which a para attack could be launched would give the Germans adequate time to blow the bridges themselves. Gale concluded that his only option was to seize the bridges by a *coup de main*, using Horsas, which could each set down twenty-eight fighting men in an instant. Best of all, in gliders they could arrive like thieves in the night, without noise or light, unseen and unheard. Gale says in his memoirs that he got the idea of a *coup de main* by studying German glider landings at the Fort of Eben Emael in Belgium in 1940, and the Corinth Canal in Greece in 1941. He was sure that if his glider pilots and his company commander were good enough, it could be done. He thought the real problem would be holding the bridges against counter-attack until the paratroopers arrived.

Gale briefed Brigadier Poett, explaining his conclusions and his reasoning. He told Poett he was putting the glider company under his, Poett's, command for the operation, because Poett's would be the para brigade that got to the gliders first. He told Poett, 'the seizing of the bridges intact is of the utmost importance to the conduct of future operations. As the bridges will have been prepared for demolition, the speedy overpowering of the bridge defences will be your first objective and it is therefore to be seized by the *coup de main* party. You must accept risks to achieve this.'

Next Gale went to Kindersley, explained his *coup de main* idea, and asked Kindersley who was the best company commander in his brigade to carry out the mission. Kindersley replied, 'I think that all my men are jolly good leaders, but I think Johnny Howard might do this one rather well.' They decided to find out if he could.

Gale laid on a major three-day exercise. D Company was assigned to capture intact three small bridges and defend them until relieved. It was a night assault, with much of the division landing all over the area. The glider troops rode in four trucks and were told by umpires riding with them when they had landed. They pranged at 2300 hours and after a brief struggle with the paras guarding the bridges, D Company managed to capture the structures before they were blown. 'We had a really first-class fight', Howard recalls, despite the blank ammunition. Windy Gale and Hugh Kindersley and Nigel Poett were all there, watching.

At the debriefing, on April 18, Gale praised the 'bridge prangers' as he called D Company, singling out for special citation the company's 'dash and verve'. That was highly pleasing for Howard and his men, of course, but what came next was even better. Colonel Mike Roberts called Howard into his office and began to bring him into the larger picture. Roberts said D Company would have a 'very important task to carry out when the invasion started. You are to capture two bridges, intact. The bridges are about a quarter of a mile apart and each is over fifty yards long.' Looking up, Roberts stared at Howard, then said, 'You will be the spearhead of the invasion, certainly the first British fighting force to land on the Continent.' Usually a non-demonstrative man who spent most of his time worrying, Roberts was deeply moved. He told Howard it was a great honour for the Ox and Bucks to provide the company for such a task.

Roberts warned Howard that all the information was Top Secret, and said he had been brought in only because Gale was laying on another, even larger exercise. This had the code name MUSH, and it would in fact be a rehearsal for D-Day for the whole of the 6th Airborne Division. Howard should approach the exercise with that in mind. Further, Gale had decided on the basis of the previous exercise to strengthen D Company from four to six platoons. Roberts told Howard to select any two platoons he wanted from the regiment.

Howard selected two platoons from B Company, one commanded by Sandy Smith, the other by Dennis Fox. Both lieutenants were keen athletes, perfectly fit, and popular with their men. Howard told Brian Priday, who knew Smith and Fox rather better, to extend the invitation; Priday pulled Smith and Fox out of their quarters one evening 'and said to us in great secrecy, "would you like to join our little party which we're going to do and we can't tell you much more than that but are you prepared to join D Company?" '

Smith and Fox looked at each other. They both thought the army a bit of a gas, and they especially disliked regular soldiers, and most of all they hated the fanatics. John Howard was the leading fanatic in the regiment. Furthermore, Fox and Smith enjoyed 'chasing women and having a good time. We were very high-spirited and that bunch of D Company officers, they used to bore the living daylights out of us. Sweeney, Brotheridge, Hooper, Priday, Wood – we didn't want to get near them. And come to that, they thought us very peculiar.' But to pass up a Top Secret special mission was unthinkable, and Smith and Fox joined up. To their surprise, they merged in with D Company immediately and without difficulty.

D Company was further reinforced by the addition of thirty sappers under Captain Jock Neilson. The sappers were Royal Engineers, but also paratroopers. Howard recalled that when they reported to him, 'those paraboys were quite definite about not landing in gliders'. Howard explains, 'There is a good healthy respect between the paraboys and the gliderboys, but I can't resist saying that whereas a high percentage of us would willingly jump out of a plane on a chute into battle, you would have to go a long way to get a glider-load of paraboys to prang into battle in a Horsa'.

Before MUSH was held, D Company got a two-week leave. Joy had by then bought a small house in Oxford, where John went to see his new-born daughter for the first time. It was on this occasion that John left his service dress uniform behind, and took Terry's baby shoe with him. On an earlier occasion, in 1940, when fear of an invasion was high, John had given her a .45 revolver and instructed her in its use. When he left after this leave, she noticed that he had taken the bullets with him. She assumed he was afraid that he might not come back and she would kill herself out of love for him. Joy couldn't even lift the pistol much less use it.

Den Brotheridge, Wally Parr and most of the other chaps managed to visit their families too.

At the end of April, everyone reported back to Bulford. All leaves were cancelled until further notice, and operation MUSH was held. D Company was to attack, capture, and hold a bridge until relieved by the paras. It was a night-time operation, and all six platoons and the sappers participated. They were driven to the site of the manoeuvre, marched a couple of miles to their supposed LZ, then told by the umpire with them to lay down and wait for his signal telling them they had pranged. They were only a few hundred yards from the bridge, which was being guarded by Polish paratroopers.

With the signal from the umpire, D Company began to move forward, silently, only to encounter barbed wire. After all the obstacle practice the company had had, cutting a way through the wire was only a moment's work. Tony Hooper was first through, and with his platoon rushed the bridge. Howard recalls, 'The Poles were firing and swearing in Polish at Tony and his chaps as they tore across the bridge, as our chaps swore back in English. Then there was a colossal bang.' The umpires declared the bridge had been blown. 'I saw Tony on the bridge arguing heatedly with an irate umpire who had put him out of action together with most of his platoon. The umpire won and the men sat disconsolate on the bridge with their helmets off.'

By then, paratroopers were rushing onto the bridge. The Poles, hopelessly outnumbered, refused to accept the umpire's decision that the bridge had been destroyed. When told in no uncertain terms that they must lay down their arms they merely said, 'No speak English' and went on scrapping. There were several little fist-fights which everyone but the harassed umpires seemed to enjoy. Several of the combatants finished in the drink.

The umpires declared that Sweeney's platoon had been put out of action by fire from Brotheridge's platoon. Sweeney had not recognised Brotheridge's men as they crept silently towards the bridge. Howard learned a lesson from the experience.

MUSH was a well-conceived and well-conducted rehearsal. The exercise revealed problems, such as mutual recognition in the dark, but it also convinced Howard, and his many superiors who watched, that if the Horsas pranged on the right spot, the *coup de main* would work.

45

The *sine qua non*, of course, was getting the Horsas down in the right place. To that end, Jim Wallwork and the Glider Pilots Regiment were working day and night, literally, on operation Deadstick. In April, 1944, Wallwork and his fellow pilots had done a demonstration for Gale, operation Skylark, landing their Horsas on a small triangle from 6,000 feet. When all the gliders were safely down, the GPR commanding officer, Colonel George Chatteron, stepped out of the bushes. He had General Gale with him. Chatteron was boasting, 'Well, Windy, there you see it, I told you my GPR boys can do this kind of thing any day.' Wallwork overheard the remark and thought, 'I wish we could, but that is a bit of asking.'

To make sure they could, Gale put them on operation Deadstick. Sixteen pilots of the GPR, two for each of the six gliders going in on D-Day plus four reserves, were posted to Tarrant Rushton in Dorset, an RAF airfield where there were two Halifax squadrons and a squadron of Horsas. The men of the GPR were treated as very special people indeed. They had their own Nissen hut, excellent food, and a captain delegated to them – they were all staff sergeants – to see to it that their every want was catered for. As Oliver Boland recalled it, 'we were the most pampered group of people in the British army at the time'.

The pilots were introduced to their tug crews, which was an innovation: previously the glider pilots had not known their tug pilots. The tug crews lived near the GPR boys at Tarrant Rushton, and they got to know each other. The glider pilots had the same crew on each training flight, and this would be the crew that tugged them on D-Day.

The training flights for operation Deadstick were hellishly difficult. Colonel Chatteron had the pilots landing beside a small L-shaped wood, a quarter of a mile long down the long end, and a few yards along the angle. The pilots landed with three gliders (carrying cement blocks for a load) going up the L and three on the blind side. In daylight, on a straight-in run, it was a snap. But then Chatteron started having them release at 7,000 feet and fly by times and courses, using a stopwatch, making two or three full turns before coming in over the wood. That was not too bad, either, because – as Wallwork explains – 'in broad daylight you can always cheat a little'. Next Chatteron put coloured glass in their flying goggles to turn day into night, and warned his pilots, 'It is silly of you to cheat on this because you've got to do it right when the time comes'. Wallwork would nevertheless whip the goggles off if he thought he was overshooting, 'but we began to play it fairly square, realising that whatever we were going to do it was going to be something important'.

By early May they were flying by moonlight, casting off at 6,000 feet, 7 miles from the wood. They flew regardless of weather. They twisted and turned around the sky, all by stopwatch. They did forty-three training flights in Deadstick altogether, more than half of them at night. They got ready.

CHAPTER FOUR

D-Day minus one month to D-Day

On May 2, Howard was summoned to 'Broadmoor', code name for Gale's planning headquarters, an old country place full of rickety stairs and low beams, near Milston on Salisbury Plain. It was surrounded by barbed wire and military police and had elaborate security precautions. Once inside, Howard was taken to Brigadier Poett's office. Explaining that D Company was being detached from the Ox and Bucks and given a special assignment, Poett handed Howard his orders. They were marked *Bigot* and *Top Secret*, and they instructed Howard 'to seize *intact* the bridges over the River Orne and canal at Benouville and Ranville, and to hold them until relief'.

The orders provided ample information on enemy dispositions that Howard could expect to encounter, a garrison of about fifty men armed with four to six light machine-guns, one or two anti-tank guns, and a heavy machine-gun. 'A concrete shelter is under construction, and the bridges will have been prepared for demolition.' There was a battalion of the 736th Grenadier Regiment in the area, with eight to twelve tanks under command, and with motor transport. At least one platoon would be prepared as a fighting patrol, ready to move out at once to seek information. Howard should expect the enemy to be 'in a high state of alertness. The bridge garrison may be standing to, and charges will have been laid in the demolition chambers.'

At this point in his reading Howard may have wondered how on earth General Gale expected him to seize intact bridges that were prepared for demolition. All the enemy had to do was press a button or move a switch and up would go the bridges. Gale himself, in his 1948 book, *The 6th Airborne Division in Normandy*, explains his thinking about this problem:

> There is always or nearly always a slip between the cup and the lip: orders are vague: there is uncertainty: has the moment arrived or should one wait? Who is the individual actually responsible both for working the switch and for ordering the bridges to be blown? These questions are age-old and on the doubts that might exist in some German mind or minds at the critical moment I based the plan. But a moment or two was all that I knew we would get. The assault on the bridges must, therefore, come like a bolt from the blue.

Howard's orders of May 2 informed him that his initial relief would come from the 5th Para Brigade, which would drop northeast of Ranville at 0050 hours and then 'move forthwith to take up a defensive position round the two bridges'. Simultaneously, 3rd Para Brigade would drop on the high wooded ground south of Le Mesnil forest. At 0600, the British 3rd Infantry Division would begin its landings west of Ouistreham 'with objective Caen'. Attached to the 3rd Division were Lord Lovat's Commandos, who would move forward as rapidly as possible to establish a land link between the beaches and the paratroopers and glider-borne troops in and around the bridges. The brigade of Commandos could be expected any time after 1100 hours.

To carry out his assignment, Howard was given his own D Company, plus two platoons from B Company, a detachment of two dozen sappers, one wing of the Glider Pilots Regiment, and six Horsa gliders. Poett's May 2 orders also gave Howard the general outline of how he should proceed: 'The capture of the bridges will be a *coup de main* operation depending largely on surprise, speed and dash for success. Provided the bulk of your force lands safely, you should have little difficulty in overcoming the known opposition on the bridges. Your difficulties will arise in holding off an enemy counter-attack on the bridges, until you are relieved.' The counter-attack should be expected any time after 0100 hours, or within an hour of landing, and the most likely line of approach for the counter-attacking force would be from the west.

Howard was ordered to organise his defensive position immediately after taking the bridges, because 'it is vital that the crossing places be held, and to do this you will secure a close bridgehead on the west bank, in addition to guarding the bridges. The immediate defence of the bridges and of the west bank of the canal must be held at all costs.' Poett's orders envisaged more than a passive defence, however. 'You will harass and delay the deployment of the enemy counter-attack

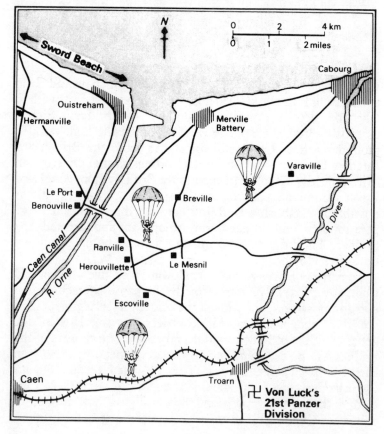

forces . . . by offensive patrols', the orders read. 'Patrols will remain mobile and offensive. Up to one third of your effective force may be used in this role. The remaining two thirds will be used for static defence and immediate counter-attack.'

Poett was also explicit in the orders as to the role of the sappers. Their sole tasks, in order of priority, were to neutralise the demolition mechanisms, remove charges from demolition chambers, and establish ferries. He also promised that one company of the 7th Para Battalion of the 5th Para Brigade would be despatched 'with the utmost possible speed', and would reach Howard's position by 0230 hours. Once there, they would come under Howard's command until arrival of the officer commanding the 7th Para Battalion.

Poett concluded his orders, 'The training of your force will be regarded as a first priority matter.' He encouraged Howard to demand special stores and training facilities, and promised every possible help.

When Howard finished reading the orders, Poett told him that he did not intend to interfere with D Company's preparation for the *coup de main*. Howard would have the twin responsibilities of designing an effective training programme, and of making the detailed plan for the seizure of the bridges.

Howard could scarcely keep his feelings to himself. He was concerned about the various challenges he faced, of course, and could imagine any number of things going wrong. But he was also exhilarated, as he had never been before in his life; and he was tremendously proud that D Company had been chosen to lead the way on D-Day.

Poett next briefed Howard on operation Overlord. Howard was amazed by the size and scope of the invading force, and impressed by the critical nature of his bridges to success on the left flank. He noted that the American paratroopers, two divisions strong, were landing on the far right flank of the invasion in the Cherbourg peninsula. By the end of the briefing, Howard says, 'I knew absolutely everything about the invasion of Europe. Where it was to be, who was taking part, how it was to be done, everything except the date.'

Poett gave Howard a green pass, which allowed him to enter Broadmoor at will. But Poett would not allow him to take away

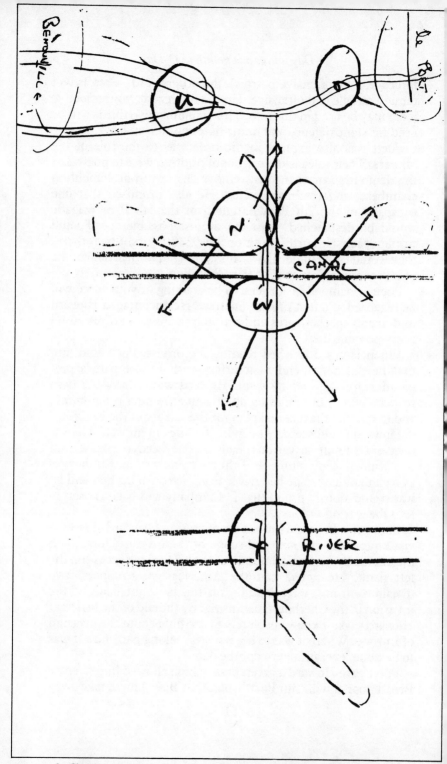

2 Sketch made by John Howard early in the planning for the Pegasus operation showing the planned disposition of the platoons if all landed on target.

his orders, the reconnaissance photographs, maps, or even notes. Nor was he allowed to tell his second-in-command, Priday, about D Company's mission, much less any of the rest of the officers. The need to keep his secret was a great strain for him.

Back at Bulford, Howard concentrated the training. Out on Salisbury Plain, he used tape to lay out a river and a canal, with two bridges over them, all at the exact distances of his real targets. Day and night, his platoons practised capturing them: sometimes one platoon, sometimes three, sometimes all six. All the exercising was controlled by radio. Howard felt that above all his plan had to be flexible. The gliders were to take off at one-minute intervals line astern, but there was absolutely no guarantee which order they would land in, or even where they would land. If only one glider hit the target, that platoon had to be prepared to do the job of all six platoons. Simultaneously, Howard worked on the men not to use their voices before the fighting began. Then, reminding them of the cost of silence in operation MUSH, Howard told them that as soon as the first shot went off, they should all start shouting their radio call signs as loudly as they could. No. 1 glider was Able, no. 2 was Baker, no. 3 was Charlie, and so on. Howard wanted the men to shout out their identifications over and over, both to identify each other and to give the Germans the feeling that the enemy was there in great numbers.

From these exercises over the taped-up bridges and roads, Howard decided that General Gale's plan for landing inside (between) the bridges rather than outside them, was correct. The LZs on the inside were awfully small, to be sure, and so situated that one group of gliders, at the canal bridge, would have to land facing north, towards the coast, the other group facing south, towards Caen, which required splitting the glider formations at take-off. These disadvantages were outweighed by two major advantages. First, the inside landing sites were smack against the bridges, instead of some distance away. Second, by having all his platoons inside, Howard could call on them to support one another.

Broadmoor, meanwhile, was collecting and putting together intelligence on the bridges and surrounding villages, and making it available to Howard. Thanks to Georges Gondrée, Madame Vion, the Resistance in Caen, and the photo reconnaissance of the RAF, there was a rather fabulous amount available. Divisional intelligence was able to tell Howard who were the collaborators in Benouville, who were Resistance. He knew, as the Germans did not, that Georges Gondrée spoke English and his wife German. He was given a complete topographical report on the area. He knew that Benouville contained 589 residents, that M. Thomas was the mayor, that the voltage was 110/200 3 phase AC – even that Madame Vion was considered something of an autocrat. He was warned that from the roof of the Château de Benouville, a three-storey maternity hospital, the Germans would have a commanding field of fire over the valley of the Orne for a considerable distance. And many in the village, Howard found out, looked sideways when Thérèse Gondrée walked past. They were suspicious of her German accent, and did not approve of the fact that she lived right next to the garrison and sold beer to the Germans.

Howard also learned from his intelligence summary that the fighting value of the garrison at the bridge had been assessed at '40 per cent static and 15 per cent in a counter-attack role. Equipment consists of an unknown proportion of French, British and Polish weapons.' The last sentence read, 'This intelligence summary will be destroyed by fire immediately after reading.'

Even though Howard could not take the air reconnaissance photographs out of Broadmoor, he could go there to study them any time he wished. The RAF people had set up a stereograph system for him to provide a three-dimensional view. He could even see down into the enemy trenches along the eastern side of the canal. Poett went over the photographs with Howard. He kept telling him that he had to capture those bridges in a few minutes, before they could be blown. The role, even the survival, of the 6th Airborne Division depended on keeping those bridges intact.

How good, and how up to date, was Howard's intelligence? As good as it could possibly be. Of all the attributes the British forces demonstrated during the Second World War, none equalled their ability to gather, evaluate, and disseminate intelligence. At this vital task, they were unquestionably the best in the world. The British government invested heavily in intelligence in all its various forms, and received a handsome return. John Howard was one of the beneficiaries. Here are three examples of what he got:

In early May, Rommel visited the bridges. He ordered an anti-tank gun emplacement built, and a pillbox ringed by barbed wire to protect it. He also ordered more slit trenches dug. Work began immediately, and within two days Howard was told by the RAF that Jerry was installing some suspicious emplacements. Within a week, word came via Gondrée through Madame Vion to Caen to SOE to Broadmoor to Howard that the gun emplacement had a 50mm anti-tank gun in it, with a roof over it, and that the pillbox was finished.

In mid-May, 21st Panzer Division moved from Brittany to Normandy, and on May 23 to the Caen area, with von Luck's regiment taking up positions just east of Caen. On May 24, Howard knew about the movement of the division. On May 25, Hickman's Independent Parachute Regiment moved into the area. Howard knew about it the next day.

The intelligence people had produced a model of the area, twelve foot square. Howard describes it as 'a work of art – every building, tree, bush and ditch, trench, fence etc. was there'. The model was changed daily, in accordance with the results of the morning reconnaissance flight. Thus on May 15 Schmidt knocked down two buildings along the canal, to give him a better field of fire. Howard saw the change on the model the next day.

Howard's visits to Broadmoor were characterised by the place's nickname, 'The Madhouse'. After clearing numerous check points with his green pass, Howard recalls going in and being struck by 'the harassed look on the faces of many people walking about the building, obviously up to their eyes in last-minute changes in major plans'.

At the end of his early May briefing, Poett had told Howard that he could have anything he needed for his training programme. Taking Poett at his word, Howard ordered up German opposition: soldiers who would defend the bridge wearing German uniforms, using German weapons and tactics, and insofar as possible shouting their orders in German. He obtained captured German weapons, so that all his men were thoroughly familiar with what they could do, and how to operate them. He had but to snap his fingers, and trucks would appear, to carry his platoons to wherever he wanted to go.

D Company got the best of everything, except in food, in which area it got no special favours. There was very strict rationing throughout the country, and the food was bad; worse, there was not enough of it. Parr recalls:

> Much of your money, spare money, went on grub. I was always hungry. You worked so hard, you trained so hard that the grub they gave you wasn't enough to keep you going and you didn't ask what it was, you just grabbed it and you just shovelled it down, as simple as that. So the first thing you got paid you used to do is make out for the NAAFI and get chow. Yeah, you supplemented your diet with your pay, there's no doubt about that.

Howard was carrying some heavy burdens, of which the chief was being the only man in the company who was 'bigoted'. Howard longed to put Brian Priday at least into the picture, partly to share the burden of knowledge, partly so that he could discuss his planning with him. He did, in fact, get permission to brief Priday around May 21.

He was pushing the men hard now, harder than ever, but no matter how he varied the order of landing or direction of attack or other aspects of the exercise, it was always the same make-believe bridges, at the same distances. Everyone was getting bored stiff. After about ten days of this, Howard called the men together on the parade ground and told them, 'Look, we are training for a special purpose'. He did not mention the invasion – he hardly had to – but he went on: 'You'll find that a lot of the training we are doing, this capturing of things like bridges, is connected with that special purpose. If any of you mention the word "bridges" outside our training hours and I get to know about it, you'll be for the high jump and your feet

won't touch before you land in the Glasshouse and get RTU.'
(Wally Parr told Irene the next evening, over the telephone,
that he would be doing bridges on D-Day.)

Von Luck, as noted, had moved to the east of Caen, between
the River Dives and the Orne River. So had Hickman. Von
Luck planned, and practised, his defences. He marked out the
routes forward to alternative assembly areas behind likely
invasion points. He laid down rest and refuelling areas, detailed
traffic control units, marked bypasses and allotted anti-aircraft
guns for road protection. Hickman meanwhile was engaging
in anti-paratrooper exercises. Even Major Schmidt, at the
bridges, was finally getting some sense of urgency. He was
completing his bunkers, and was almost ready to get around to
putting in the anti-glider poles. The Gondrées watched all this,
and said nothing, except to Madame Vion.

Howard asked the topographical people to search the map of
Britain and find him some place where a river and a canal ran
closely together and were crossed by bridges on the same road.
They found such a spot outside Exeter. Howard moved the
company down there, and for six days, by day and by night,
attacked those Exeter bridges. Townspeople came to gape as
the lads dashed about, throwing grenades, setting off explosives, getting into hand-to-hand combat, cursing, yelling,
'Able, Able', or 'Easy, Easy' at the top of their lungs. Howard
had them practise every possible development he could imagine
– only one glider getting down, or the gliders landing out of
proper sequence, or the dozens of other possibilities. He taught
every man the basic rudiments of the sappers' jobs; he
instructed the sappers in the functions of the platoons; he made
certain that each of his officers was prepared to take command
of the whole operation, and sergeants and corporals to take
command of each platoon, if need be.

Howard insisted that they all become proficient in putting
together and using the canvas boats that they were bringing
along in the event the bridges were blown. Assault boat training
was 'always good for morale,' according to Howard, because
'somebody inevitably went overboard and that poor individual
never failed to make sure he wasn't the only one who got wet'.

The hurling about of grenades and thunder-flashes caused some problems and brought some fun. Thunder-flashes were tossed into the river, to provide fish for supper. The local Council protested at this illegal fishing. The Council also protested that all this running back and forth over its bridges, and all these explosives going off, were seriously weakening the structures. (They stand, solid, today.) A homeowner in the area had some tiles blown off his roof by a mortar smoke bomb. Irate, he confronted Howard, who passed him along to Priday, who gave him the proper forms to fill in so that he could get the tiles replaced. One month later, sitting in a foxhole in Normandy, Priday let out a whoop of laughter. The mail had been delivered, and in it was a letter from the homeowner, demanding to know when his roof would be fixed.

Out of all this practice and after consulting with his officers, Howard made his final plan. The key to it was to put the pillbox out of action while simultaneously getting a platoon onto the other side of the bridge. It had to be accomplished before shots were fired, if possible, and certainly before the Germans were fully aroused. The pillbox was a key not only because of its firing power, but because – according to information received from Georges Gondrée – that was the location of the button that could blow the bridge. Howard detailed three men from no. 1 glider (Brotheridge's platoon) to dash to the pillbox and throw grenades through the gun-slits. To take physical possession of the opposite bank, Howard detailed Brotheridge to lead the remainder of his platoon on a dash across the bridge. Ideally, Howard wanted Brotheridge to hear the thuds of the grenades in the pillbox as he was mid-way across the bridge.

No. 2 glider, David Wood's platoon, would clear up the inner defences, the trenches, machine-gun nests and anti-tank gun pit along the east bank. No. 3 glider, Sandy Smith's platoon, would cross the bridge to reinforce Brotheridge. On the river bridge, the procedure would be the same, with Priday in no. 4 glider (Hooper's platoon), Sweeney in no. 5, and Fox in no. 6. All six platoons were trained to do all six of the platoon tasks.

Each glider would carry five sappers, the thirty men under

the command of Captain R. K. Jock Neilson. The sappers' main job was to move immediately to the bridges, then hand-over-hand themselves along the bottom beams, cutting fuses and disposing of explosives.

If all went well at both bridges, Howard intended to call two platoons from the river bridge over to the canal bridge, sending one towards Benouville as a fighting patrol, and holding the other in reserve. This was because the threat he faced lay to the west. That was German-occupied territory, with a garrison of some sort in every village. The first counter-attack was likely to come from the west, possibly led by tanks. To the east, the 6th Airborne Division would be dropping thirty minutes later and setting up in Ranville to provide protection in that direction.

The landing operation was John Howard's plan. His superiors let him work it out himself, then approved his final presentation. He ran through it again and again, until the men were exhausted and almost too tense and too bored to care any longer.

But each time he ran through it, Howard saw something he had overlooked. One day, for example, he stopped an exercise and said he had been thinking, that if so and so happened, and such and such, I'd need volunteers to swim the canal with a Bren gun to set up flanking fire, or to create a diversion with explosives. As Howard remembers the occasion, 'competition for this hazardous mission was high'. As Parr remembers it, he raised his hand before Howard could call for volunteers. Howard impatiently told him to put it down. Parr waved it some more. 'Oh, all right Parr, what is it?' Parr replied that since Billy Gray and Charlie Gardner were the two strongest swimmers, perhaps they should get this detail. 'Good idea, Parr', Howard pronounced, and it was done. Parr spent the remainder of the week staying far away from Gray and Gardner.

The last night in Exeter was a classic eve-of-battle event. Howard gave the men the evening off, and they poured into and out of Exeter's pubs. There were fights, windows were broken. The Chief of Police got Howard on the phone, and he and Priday jumped into a jeep and tore into Exeter, about three miles away. 'As we crossed the bridge we were picked up by the police for speeding', recalls Howard, 'and we arrived at the station with police escort'. Howard went straight to the Chief's office and said, 'If you find Lieutenant Brotheridge he will soon tell you how to get the troops back'. Then Howard noticed the Chief's World War I medals, 'and I knew the type of chap I was talking to, and I explained to him in confidence that this was likely to be our last night out; his attitude was absolutely wonderful'. The Chief called out the entire force on duty at the time and put it to rounding up D Company and escorting it, gently, back to its transport and encampment.

Brotheridge, in fact, turned out to be no help, although Howard had sent him along with the men specifically to exert a good influence. But he was too much the footballer, too much like the men, to stay sober on a night like this. Besides, he had a lot on his mind, and he needed some mental relief. His baby was due in less than a month, but he could not expect to see his wife before then, and who could tell about afterwards? He was proud that John had chosen him to lead the first platoon across the canal bridge, but he had to be realistic – everyone knew that the first man over that bridge was the man most likely to get shot. Not killed, necessarily, but almost certainly shot. That first man was equally likely to have the bridge blow up in his face.

To escape such thoughts, Brotheridge had gone drinking with his sergeants, and when Howard arrived was drunk. Howard and Priday drove him back to camp, while the trucks took the men home. The people of Exeter, and their Police Chief, never made a complaint.

In late May, D Company moved to Tarrant Rushton. In a wired-in encampment on this huge base, completely secured, the company met Jim Wallwork, John Ainsworth, Oliver Boland, and the other glider-pilots. Howard immediately found them impressive and was pleased to note that they were absorbed into the company as family members as quickly as the sappers had been.

How dependent D Company was on the pilots became quickly apparent after arrival in Tarrant Rushton. Now that the company was properly sealed in, Howard was free to give his briefing. First to the officers, then to the men, he explained the operation.

Howard covered the walls of the Nissen briefing hut with photographs of the bridges, and had the model in the middle of the room. As he talked, the eyes of the officers and men opened wider and wider – at the amount of intelligence available to them, at the crucial nature of their task, and at the idea of being the first men to touch the soil of France. But what they also noted was the extreme smallness of the LZs, especially on the canal bridge. Having examined the German trench system, and discussed the Germans' weapons and emplacements, the officers – and later the men – were completely confident that they could take the bridges intact. They could, that is, if – and only if – the pilots put them down on the right spots.

The pilots were now into the last days of Deadstick. Calling on the British movie industry for help, the Air Ministry had put together a film. By flipping through thousands of photographs, each ever so slightly different, the producers made a 'moving picture' that depicted the actual flight the pilots would make on D-Day. There was a running commentary.

'The viewer felt as if he were in the cockpit and flying the thing', Wallwork recalls. The commentary told altitude, air speed, bearing, location. When the glider cast off, 'you got the whole sensation of diving a thousand feet and seeing the fields of France coming up towards you'. Level off, check your bearing, turn, check your bearing, turn again, then the bridges were in view. 'You come into this fly-in,' as Wallwork describes the film, 'and you are still on this bearing and the next thing you saw was the tower of the bridge getting nearer and nearer and then the film cuts out as you crash'. The pilots could see the film whenever they wanted, and they watched it often. In his orders Howard had been given very strict instructions about *not* using the glider pilots in any combatant role. He therefore gave them the task of unloading the gliders after the platoons had landed and attacked in light fighting order. The pilots were then to carry the ammunition, heavy equipment, etc. up to their respective platoons. Howard was well aware that it was a job they would not like at all; he knew only too well that they were the type who would want to join in the initial assault and take part in any ensuing battle. But the pilots *had* to be got back to England unscathed so as to be able to fly the 1st Airborne Division into action.

Howard briefed the men over and over, by sections and by platoons. He encouraged them to go into the hut whenever they wished, examine the maps and the photographs and the model, and talk among themselves about their particular tasks.

On May 29, he called the reinforced company together and issued escape aids, 'very Boy Scoutish things', Howard says. They included a metal file to be sewn into the battle smock, a brass pants button that had been magnetised, so that when balanced on a pin-head it became a tiny compass, a silk scarf with the map of France on it, water-purifying tablets, and French francs. 'This sort of thing absolutely thrilled the troops to bits', Howard recalls: 'I have never seen such enthusiasm about such simple things like that'. Billy Gray remembers that all the French money was gambled away in two hours.

All the officers were issued with more sophisticated escape wallets. They included large wads of French francs, which were all conveniently 'lost in battle'. Howard says he lost his francs playing poker with a popular Army Padre.

That night, in Normandy, von Luck was conducting exercises, designed to counter any landing, even commando, by an immediate counter-attack. That day, Major Schmidt received a shipment of slave labourers from the Todt Organization and put them to work digging holes for anti-glider poles, in what he figured were the most likely LZs for gliders. He began with the areas around his bridges. The poles themselves had not yet arrived, but were expected daily.

On May 30, when Howard and all of D Company saw the photographic evidence of the holes, their first reaction was that somehow the great secret had got out, that the Germans knew where they were coming. Kindersley came down to visit Howard, guessing correctly that Howard would be in a blue mood. 'I know about those photographs', he began, 'but there is nothing to worry about'. Howard voiced his fear: all those photographs taken by the RAF for the movie for the pilots, all those photographs each morning, surely the Germans must have figured out that the bridges were to be attacked because of all the reconnaissance activity. Kindersley laughed encouragingly. 'John', he said, 'we're taking similar photographs of every bridge or target between the Bay of Biscay and Dunkirk'.

That relieved one worry. Howard went to Wallwork with the other worry. 'Supposing the poles are put into the holes before we land? What will our chances be?'

'That's just what we want, sir', Wallwork answered.

'What do you mean? What can you mean?' Howard asked.

Wallwork explained that the gliders would be overloaded, flying into a narrow field with an embankment at one end. They would be landing in the direction of the embankment, and Wallwork was worried about hitting that. He continued, 'Now, those poles will take something off one wing, and something off the other wing – it's just damned cheap plywood, you know – and will pull us up absolutely beautifully'.

Howard's face brightened. 'Right', he said, 'well, let's get the company on parade'. He called the men together, let them mumble and rumble awhile as they studied the aerial photographs, mostly about those holes, then explained to them what the Brigadier had told him about photographing everywhere, not just their bridges, and then asked Wallwork to tell the company what he had just said about the poles being exactly what was needed. Wallwork did so, and the men were satisfied.

'Put it down to ignorance', Wally Parr explains, 'call it what you like, we could see the situation. But Johnny Howard said it could be done and Wallwork said we could do it and that was the end of the subject. If Johnny Howard said we could do it, we could do it.'

Besides the poles, Wallwork had to worry about Howard's request that he break through the barbed wire with the nose of his Horsa, a difficult enough task with an unloaded glider in daylight on a runway. And his glider – all the gliders – was badly overloaded, with thirty or thirty-one men in each, plus ammunition. There were also two canvas assault boats per glider. The sappers had heavy equipment. The men were carrying up to twenty pounds more ammunition each than had been allotted, and still were trying to add more to their load.

Wallwork told Howard that the extra weight would increase air speed, and thus landing speed. They would need a longer landing area than was available. Howard told Captain Neilson of the Royal Engineers to get rid of some weight by dropping off one sapper per glider, but Neilson convinced Howard that he absolutely had to have all his sappers. Howard removed one boat from each glider. Not enough, Wallwork told him. Six hundred more pounds per glider had to go.

Howard reluctantly made his decision. Two privates from each platoon would have to drop out. It was a 'terrible decision', he recalls. He gave it to his platoon commanders and told them to select the men to be left behind. In Brotheridge's platoon, Billy Gray says, 'We all started shouting, "Parr's married, let Parr drop out. Let's get rid of Parr!" And Wally immediately did his nut, and he was allowed to stay.'

The lieutenants made the choices. The next day, Howard says, 'I had men asking to see me at company office and crying their eyes out; a big, tough, bloody airborne soldier crying his eyes out asking not to be left behind. It was an awful moment for them.'

At one of his briefings, Howard had as usual asked for questions. 'Sir', someone piped up, 'can't we have a doctor. We are going in on our own and all.' Howard thought that an excellent idea, asked Poett if he could get a volunteer from the divisional medical staff, and John Vaughan, an RAMC captain, came to join D Company. That meant another private had to be bumped, but fortunately, a soldier in Smith's platoon had sprained his ankle playing football.

Vaughan has a nice anecdote to illustrate Howard's exuberance in the last days before the invasion. On May 31 Vaughan and Howard drove to Broadmoor, Howard driving much too fast as he always did. When they arrived, who should be standing there as Howard screeched the brakes, but Brigadier Poett. Howard leaped out of the jeep, did a full somersault, and came down directly in front of Poett. He snapped into attention, gave a full and quite grand salute, and shouted, 'Sir!'

That same night, Smith and Fox sneaked out of Tarrant

Rushton (neither of them can recall how they managed it) to have dinner in a local hotel with their girlfriends (both remember the meal and the girls vividly).

That evening, Wallwork and the other pilots were given a special set of orders. These said that the bearer was not responsible to anyone, that he was to be returned to the UK by the most expeditious means, and that this order overruled all other orders. It was signed by General Montgomery himself. Poett also told Howard privately, 'Whatever you do, John, don't let those pilots get into combat. They are much too valuable to be wasted. Get them back here.'

On June 3, Howard got his last intelligence report. Major Schmidt had completed his defences; his trenches along the canal bank were done, as was the pillbox, and the anti-tank gun was in place. The garrison consisted of about fifty men, armed with four to six light machine-guns, one anti-aircraft machine-gun, an anti-tank gun, and a heavy machine-gun in its own pillbox. A maze of tunnels connected the underground bunkers and the fighting posts. More buildings had been torn down to open fields of fire. The anti-glider poles appeared to have arrived, but were not in place yet.

That same day, Monty himself came through Tarrant Rushton. He asked to see the gliders and John Howard. He wanted to know if Major Howard thought he could pull off the *coup de main*, and he was obviously acquainted with details of the operation. Howard assured him that the job would be done. Monty's parting remark was, 'Get as many of the chaps back as you can'.

General Gale paid a visit. He gathered his airborne troops around him and gave them his version of an inspirational talk. Jack Bailey can only recall one line: Gale said that 'the German today is like the June bride. He knows he is going to get it, but he doesn't know how big it is going to be.'

June 4 was to be the day, or rather the evening, to go. D Company was primed for it, aching to get going. Everyone got into battle dress in the afternoon, checked weapons and equipment and prepared to go to the gliders, but soon after midday word came down that the mission was off. Cancellation had been half-expected, what with the high winds and heavy rains sweeping the countryside, but it was still a major disappointment. John Howard wrote in his diary, 'The weather's broken – what cruel luck. I'm more downhearted than I dare show. Wind and rain, how long will it last? The longer it goes on, the more prepared the Huns will be, the greater the chance of obstacles on the LZ. Please God it'll clear up tomorrow.'

Parr and his gang went to the movies and saw *Stormy Weather* with Lena Horne and Fats Waller. The officers gathered in David Wood's room and polished off two bottles of whisky. Twice Den Brotheridge fell into a depressed mood, and Wood could hear him reciting a poem that began, 'If I should die . . .' But his spirits soon recovered.

The following morning, June 5, the officers and men checked and rechecked their weapons. At noon, Howard told them that it was on, that they should rest, eat, and then dress for battle. The meal was fatless, to cut down on air sickness. Not much of it was eaten. Wally Parr says 'I think everybody had gone off of grub for the first time possibly in years'.

Towards evening the men got into trucks to drive to their gliders. They were a fearsome sight. They each had a rifle, a Sten gun, or a Bren gun, six to nine grenades, four Bren gun magazines. Some had mortars, one in each platoon had a wireless set strapped to his chest. They had all used black cork or burnt coke to blacken their faces. (One of the two black men in the company looked at Parr when Parr handed him some cork and said, 'I don't think I'll bother'.) All of them, officers and men, were so fully loaded that if they had fallen over it might have been impossible to get up without help. (Each infantryman weighed 250 pounds, instead of the allotted 210.) Parr called out that the sight of them alone would be enough to scare the Germans out of their wits.

As the trucks drove towards the gliders, Billy Gray can remember 'the WAAFs and the NAAFI girls along the runway, crying their eyes out'. On the trucks, the men were given their code words. The recognition signal was V, to be answered by 'for Victory'. Code word for the successful capture of the canal bridge was Ham, for the river bridge Jam. Jack meant the canal bridge had been captured but destroyed, Lard the same for the river bridge. Ham and Jam. D Company liked the sound of it, and as the men got out of their trucks they began shaking hands and saying, 'Ham and Jam, Ham and Jam'.

Howard called them together. 'It was an amazing sight', he remembers. 'The smaller chaps were visibly sagging at the knees under the amount of kit they had to carry.' He tried to give an inspiring talk, but as he confesses, 'I am a sentimental man at heart, for which reason I don't think I am a good soldier. I found offering my thanks to these chaps – a devil of a job. My voice just wasn't my own.'

Howard gave up the attempt at inspiration and told the men to load up. The officers shepherded them aboard, although not before every man, except Billy Gray, took a last-minute pee. Wally Parr chalked 'Lady Irene' on the side of Wallwork's glider. As the officers fussed over the men outside, those inside their gliders began settling in. One private bolted out of his glider and ran off into the night. Later, at his court-martial, the private explained that he had had an unshakeable premonition of his own death in a glider crash.

The officers got in last. Before climbing aboard, Brotheridge went back to Smith's glider, shook Smith's hand, and said, 'See you on the bridge, Sandy'.

Howard went round to each glider, shook hands with the platoon leader, then called out some words of cheer. He had just spoken to the Wing Commander of the Halifax squadron, he said, who had told him, 'John, don't worry about flak; we are going through a flak gap over Cabourg, one that we have been using to fly supplies into the Resistance and to bring information and agents out'.

Finally Howard, wearing a pistol and carrying a Sten gun, climbed into his own glider, closed the door and sat down next to Brotheridge. He nodded to Wallwork. Wallwork told the Halifax pilot that everything was go. At 22.56 hours, June 5, they took off, the other gliders following at one-minute intervals.

At Vimont, east of Caen, Colonel von Luck had just come in

from an exercise, and after a bite to eat sat down to do paperwork. In Ranville, Major Schmidt enjoyed his wine and his companion. At the canal bridge, Private Bonck thought with relief that there was only an hour to go and he was finished for the night. In the bunker, Private Romer groaned in his sleep, aware that he would have to get up soon to go on duty.

Sergeant Hickman drove eastwards over the bridge, identifying himself to Bonck. He was setting off for the coast to pick up the four young soldiers. As he passed the Gondrée café, he regretted that the curfew was in force. He had stopped in at the place the other day and rather liked it.

At the café, the Gondrées went to bed. In Oxford, Joy Howard did the same. In London's East End, Irene Parr stayed up. She could hear planes gathering, and it sounded bigger than anything she had ever heard before.

CHAPTER FIVE

D-Day: 0016 to 0026 hours

Wallwork struggled with his great wooden bird, swooping silently alongside the canal, below the horizon, unseen and unheard. He was trying to control the exact instant at which the Horsa lost her contest with gravity. Wally Parr glanced out the open door and, 'God Almighty, the trees were doing ninety miles an hour. I just closed my eyes and went up in my guts.' Wallwork could see the bridge looming ahead of him, the ground rushing up, trees to his left, a soft, marshy pond to his right. He could see the barbed wire straight ahead. He was going too fast, and was in danger of ploughing up against the road embankment. He was going to have to use the chute, a prospect he dreaded: 'We didn't fancy those things at all. We knew they were highly dangerous, nothing but gadgets really, never tested.' But if he were to stop in time, he would have to use it.

At the same time he was worried about the chute stopping him too quickly and leaving him short of his objective. He wanted to get as far up the LZ as possible, into the barbed wire if he could, 'not because Howard wanted me to, not because I was particularly brave or awfully skilled, but because I didn't want to be rear-rammed by no. 2 or no. 3 coming in behind me.'

As the wheels touched ground, Wallwork yelled at Ainsworth, 'Stream!' Ainsworth pushed the button, the chute billowed out, 'and by golly it lifted the tail and shoved the nose wheel down'. The whole glider then bounced back up into the air, all three wheels now torn off. 'But the chute drew us back, knocked the speed down tremendously, so in two seconds or less I told Ainsworth, "Jettison", so Ainsworth pressed the tit and away went the parachutes and we were only going along possibly at 60 mph.'

The Horsa hit ground again, this time on its skids, which threw up hundreds of friction sparks from the rocks; Howard and the other passengers thought these were tracer bullets, that they had been seen and were being fired upon. Suddenly, Howard recalls, 'there was the most hellish din imaginable, the most God Almighty crash'. The nose had buried itself in the barbed wire and crumbled.

The crash sent Wallwork and Ainsworth flying forward. They were still strapped in but their seats had broken loose and they went right out the cockpit and onto the ground. They were thus the first Allied troops to touch French soil on D-Day. Both, however, were unconscious.

Inside the glider the troops, the sappers, and the company commander were also unconscious. Howard had broken through his seat belt and was thrown against the roof beams, which jammed his helmet down over his ears and knocked him out. Private Denis Edwards thought he was dead.

Save for an occasional low moan, there was complete silence. Private Romer, pacing on the bridge, heard the crash, but assumed it was a piece of wing or tail from a crippled British bomber, a not-unusual occurrence. He went on pacing.

D Company had achieved complete surprise. Wallwork and Ainsworth had taken no. 1 platoon and set it down where it was supposed to be. Their magnificent performance was praised by Air Vice Marshal Leigh-Mallory, commanding the Allied air forces on D-Day, as the greatest feat of flying of World War II.

But with all the men knocked out, no. 1 platoon was in danger. Romer was turning at the west end of the bridge, beginning to pace towards the east. If he noticed the glider sitting there, not fifty yards from the east end of the bridge, and if he gave the alarm, and if the men in the machine-gun pillbox woke quickly enough, Howard and his men would be wiped out inside the Horsa.

To the men in the glider, it seemed afterwards that they must have been out for minutes. Each man was struggling to regain

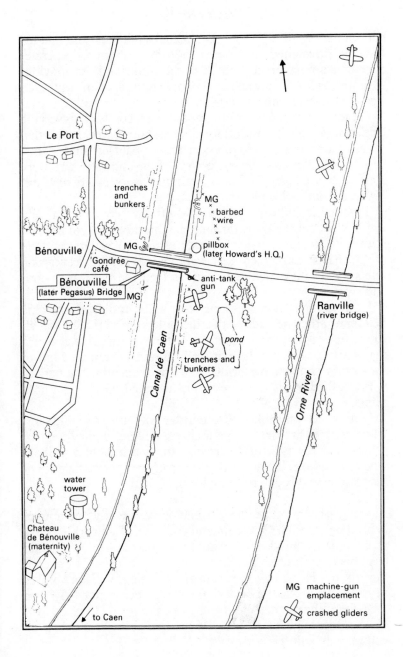

Le Port

trenches
and
bunkers

MG
× barbed
× wire
×
×
×

MG

Bénouville

○ pillbox
(later Howard's H.Q.)

Gondrée
café

Bénouville
(later Pegasus) Bridge MG

anti-tank
gun

Ranville
(river bridge)

pond

trenches and
bunkers

Canal de Caen

Orne River

water
tower

Chateau
de Bénouville
(maternity)

→ to Caen

MG machine-gun
emplacement

crashed gliders

consciousness, dimly aware that he had a job to do and that his life was threatened. It seemed to each of them a desperate, time-consuming process to clear the mind and get moving. Minutes, at least, they all recall – three minutes some say, even five minutes according to others.

In fact, they came to within eight or ten seconds. This was the critical moment, the pay-off for all those hours, weeks, months, years of training. Their physical fitness paid off first – they shook their collective heads, got rid of the cobwebs, and were alert, eager to go. Few heavyweight boxers could have recovered from such a blow so quickly.

Then their endless training paid off, as they automatically unbuckled, cut their way through the smashed door, or hopped out the back. Once again it seemed to Parr, Bailey, Gray and the others that chaos reigned, that everyone was getting in everyone else's way as they tried to get out. In fact, the exit was smooth and swift.

Howard thought he was injured or blind until he pushed his helmet up; then he realised that he could see and that he was all right. Feeling a wave of relief, he watched with pride as No. 1 platoon went through its exit drill. Howard scrambled out of the debris and saw the bridge looming over him, the barbed wire crushed at his feet. He was exhilarated. God bless those pilots.

Not a word was spoken. Brotheridge got Bailey and told him, whispering in his ear, 'Get your chaps moving'. Bailey and two others had the task of destroying the machine-gun pillbox. They moved off. Then Brotheridge gathered the remainder of his platoon and began running for the bridge.

At that moment, glider no. 2 came down, exactly one minute behind no. 1. Pilot Oliver Boland could see Wallwork's Horsa ahead of him, 'and I didn't want to run up his arse', so Boland used his chute and hit his spoilers hard, forcing his Horsa onto the ground. He had to swerve, to avoid hitting Wallwork and as he did so he broke the back of the glider. He stopped right on the edge of the pond, a bit shaken but conscious. He called over his shoulder to his passengers, 'We're here, piss off and do what you're paid to do'.

The platoon commander, David Wood, was thrown out of the glider by the impact along with his bucket of grenades and his Sten, bayonet fixed. (The bayonets had been sharpened back at Tarrant Rushton, an overly dramatic gesture on John Howard's part, many of the men thought.) His platoon gathered around him, exactly as it was supposed to do, and he went forward to where Howard was waiting, just by the perimeter wire.

Howard and his wireless operator were lying on the ground, having just been shot at by a rifleman in the trenches on the other side of the road. Howard whispered to Wood, 'no. 2 task'. That meant to clear the trenches on the eastern or near side of the road. According to Howard, 'Like a pack of unleashed hounds Wood's platoon followed him across the road and into the fray.' As they did so, no. 3 glider crash-landed.

Like no. 1, no. 3 bounced, streamed its chute, and came back down on its skids with a resounding crash. Doc Vaughan, riding just behind the pilots, was thrown straight through the cockpit; his last thought was what a bloody fool he had been to volunteer for these damned gliders. He ended up some feet in front of the glider, really knocked out – it was well over fifteen minutes before he came to.

Lieutenant Sandy Smith was beside him. 'I went shooting straight past those two pilots, through the whole bloody lot, shot out like a bullet, and landed in front of the glider.' He was stunned, covered with mud, had lost his Sten gun, and 'didn't really know what the bloody hell I was doing'. Pulling himself up on his knees, Smith looked up and into the face of one of his section leaders. 'Well', the corporal said quietly, 'what are we waiting for, sir?'

'And this', as Smith analyses the event forty years later, 'is where the training comes in'. He staggered to his feet, grabbed a Sten gun, and started moving towards the bridge. Half a dozen of his men were still trapped inside the crashed glider; one of them drowned in the pond, the only casualty of the landing. It was 0018.

On the bridge, Private Romer had just passed his fellow sentry at the mid-point and was approaching the eastern end as

Brotheridge and his platoon came rushing up the embankment. Just then a shot aimed at Howard broke the silence, and Romer saw twenty-two British airborne troops, apparently coming from out of nowhere. With their camouflaged battle smocks, their faces grotesquely blacked, they gave the most eerie sensation of blending savagery and civilisation. The civilisation was represented by the Stens and Brens and Enfields they carried at their hips, ready to fire.

They were coming at Romer at a steady trot, as determined a group as Romer thought he would ever encounter. Romer could see in a flash, by the way the men carried their weapons, by the look in their eyes and by the way their eyes darted around, all white behind the black masks, that they were highly-trained killers who were determined to have their way that night. Who was he to argue with them, a sixteen-year-old schoolboy who scarcely knew how to fire his rifle.

Romer turned and ran back towards the west end, shouting 'Paratroopers!' at the other sentry as he passed him. That sentry pulled out his Very pistol and fired a flare; Brotheridge gave him a full clip from his Sten and cut him down. The first German had just died in defence of Hitler's Fortress Europe.

Simultaneously, Bailey and his comrades tossed grenades into the apertures of the machine-gun pillbox. There was an explosion, then great clouds of dust. When it settled, Bailey found no one living inside. He ran across the bridge, to take up his position near the café.

The sappers, by this time, were beginning to inspect the bridge for explosives, and were already cutting fuses and wires.

Sergeant Hickman was driving into Le Port. He had almost arrived at the T junction, where he would make a left turn to go over the bridge, when he heard Brotheridge's Sten. Hickman told his driver to stop. He knew immediately that the gun was a Sten by its distinctive, easily recognisable rate of fire. Grabbing his Schmeisser, Hickman motioned to two of his privates to get on one side of the road leading to the bridge, while he and the other two privates moved down the left side.

Romer's shout, the Very pistol, and Brotheridge's Sten gun combined to pull the German troops manning the machine-gun

pits and slit trenches into full alert. The privates, all conscripted foreigners, began edging away, but the NCOs, all
Germans, opened fire with their MG 34 and their Schmeissers.

Brotheridge, almost across the bridge, pulled a grenade out
of his pouch and threw it at the machine-gun to his right. As he
did so, he was knocked over by the impact of a bullet in his neck.
Running just behind him came Billy Gray, his Bren gun at his
hip. Billy also fired at the sentry with the Very pistol, then
began firing towards the machine-guns. Brotheridge's grenade
went off, wiping out one of the gun pits; Gray's Bren, and shots
from others crossing the bridge, knocked out the other.

Gray was standing on the end of the bridge, on the northwest
corner. Brotheridge was lying in the middle of the road, at the
western end of the bridge. Other men in the section were
running over the bridge. Wally Parr was with them, Charlie
Gardner beside him. In the middle of the bridge, Parr suddenly
stopped. He was trying to yell 'Able, Able', as the men around
him had started doing as soon as the shooting broke out. But to
his horror, 'my tongue was stuck to the roof of my mouth and I
couldn't spit sixpence. My mouth had dried up and my tongue
was stuck.'

Attempts to yell only made the sticking worse, and his
frustration was a terrible thing to behold. His face was a fiery
red, even through the burnt cork, from the choking and from
his anger. With a great effort of will, Parr finally broke his
tongue loose and shouted, 'COME OUT AND FIGHT YOU
SQUARE-HEADED BASTARDS'. Pleased with himself,
Parr started yelling 'Ham and Jam, Ham and Jam', as he ran the
rest of the way, then turned left to go after the bunkers that
were his task.

The moon emerged from behind the clouds. As it did, Sergeant
Hickman crept to within fifty metres of the bridge. He saw no. 1
platoon coming over:

> . . . and they even frightened me, the way they charged, the
> way they fired, the way they ran across the bridge. I'm not a
> coward, but at that moment I got frightened. If you see a para
> platoon in full cry, they frighten the daylights out of you.

75

And at night-time when you see a para running with a Bren gun, and the next with a Sten, and no cover round my back, just me and four youngsters who had never been in action, so I could not rely on them – in those circumstances, you get scared. It's my own poor little life there. So I pull my trigger, I fire.

He fired at Billy Gray, reloading his Bren by the corner of the bridge. Billy finished reloading and fired a clip back. Both men were shooting from the hip, and both were pointing their guns just a bit too high, so each sent a full clip over the other man's head. While Hickman put another clip into his Schmeisser and started spraying the bridge, Billy popped into the barn on his right. As soon as he got inside, Billy rested his Bren gun on the wall and did his Jimmy Riddle.

Hickman, meanwhile, had run out of ammunition, and besides he was furious with the bridge garrison, which was hardly putting up a fight at all. He was scornful of such troops – 'they had a cushy life, all the war years in France. Never been in danger, only did guard duty.' The British, Hickman concluded, had caught them napping, and he decided to get out of there. Motioning to his four privates, he got back to the staff car and sped towards Caen, going the long way around to get to his headquarters, which were only a few kilometres straight east. Thus Hickman was the first German to pay the price for the capture of the bridge: what should have been a ten- or fifteen-minute ride took him six hours (because he had to work his way around bombed-out Caen), and by the time he arrived at his headquarters to report the landing, his major had long since been informed.

As Hickman turned to leave, Smith came running across the catwalk on the south side of the bridge, huffing more than he was running because he had wrenched his knee in the crash. Brotheridge's men were throwing grenades and firing their weapons, there was some German return fire. When Smith got to the other side, he saw a German throwing a stick grenade at him. As the German turned to leap over the low courtyard wall in the front of the café, Smith gave him a burst with his Sten

Oblique aerial reconnaissance photograph taken 24 March 1944, showing the river and canal bridge, with the beaches where the landings took place in the distance. Pegasus Bridge is on the left.

Overhead aerial reconnaissance photograph, taken 30 May 1944, showing Pegasus Bridge below the river bridge. The white lines in the surrounding fields are holes dug for 'asparagus' anti-glider poles.

3   John Howard, 1942.

4   General Omar Bradley awarding Brigadier Nigel Poett the Silver Star in recognition of the 5th Parachute Brigade's taking and holding of Pegasus Bridge; 9 June 1944.

5   Captain Brian Priday, second-in-command of D Company.

6   Jim Wallwork, pilot of No. 1 glider.

7 (*above, left*) Joy Howard, 1942.

8 (*above*) John Howard at Brotheridge's grave, Rainville, 1946.

9 (*left*) Lieutenant 'Den' Brotheridge, the first Allied soldier killed in action on D-Day.

10 Aircraft towing Horsa glider.

11 Gliders abandoned north of Rainville.

No. 1 glider with Pegasus Bridge beyond. Visible on the right is a bit of the barbed-wire ce that the pilot, Jim Wallwork, had been asked to aim for.

No. 1 glider viewed from the other end, with John Howard leaning against it at left. Wallwork ped without serious injuries, despite the smashed nose of the glider.

14 (*above*) Aerial reconnaissance photograph taken at six on D-Day showing three glid No. 1 glider is only yards fr Pegasus Bridge. The 'asparag holes are clearly visible on photograph.

15 Aerial reconnaissance phe graph showing No. 5 glider r the river bridge.

Pegasus Bridge with the Gondrée cafe at left. The German gun used by Wally Parr can be in the centre of the photograph.

| THIS WAS THE FIRST HOUSE IN FRANCE TO BE LIBERATED DURING THE LAST HOUR OF 5TH JUNE 1944 BY MEN OF THE OXFORDSHIRE & BUCKINGHAMSHIRE LIGHT INFANTRY IN THE BRITISH 6TH AIRBORNE DIVISION UNDER THE COMMAND OF MAJOR R. JOHN HOWARD | 1ÈRE MAISON DE FRANCE LIBÉRÉE DANS LA DERNIÈRE HEURE DU 5 JUIN 1944 PAR LA OXFORDSHIRE & BUCKINGHAMSHIRE LIGHT INFANTRY DE LA 6E DIVISION AÉROPORTÉE BRITANNIQUE SOUS LES ORDRES DU MAJOR R. JOHN HOWARD |

Monsieur and Madame Gondrée outside their cafe. (This book uses British time: the French e one hour ahead)

18 The pay-off: a British tank crosses Pegasus Bridge on 7 June.

19 Low-level oblique aerial reconnaissance photograph taken 24 March 1944, showing Pegasus Bridge in the centre of the picture.

gun. The German slumped over the wall, dead. Simultaneously the grenade went off. Smith did not feel anything, but his corporal came up to inquire, 'Are you all right, sir?' Smith noticed holes in his battle smock and his trousers. Then he looked at his wrist. All the flesh had been torn away, there was nothing but bone. Smith's first thought was, 'Christ, no more cricket.' Curiously, his trigger finger still worked.

Georges Gondrée had wakened at the noise. Crawling on his hands and knees, he got to the window ledge and peered over. Smith looked up from his wrist at the movement, saw Gondrée's head, swung the Sten towards him and let go a burst. He pointed the Sten too high and merely shattered the window; bullets tore into the wooden beams, but they did not hit Gondrée, who beat a hasty retreat and took his family down into the basement.

When Private Bonck heard the first shots, he pulled on his clothes, grabbed his rifle, and dashed out of the brothel and onto the street. His comrade was already there, and together they ran down to the T junction. After one look at the fire-fight going on, they turned and ran back through Benouville on the road to Caen. When they ran out of breath they stopped, talked over the situation, and fired off all their ammunition. Then they ran back to Benouville, there to report breathlessly that British troops were on the bridge and that they had expended all their ammunition before hurrying back to report.

At 0019 Brigadier Poett hit the ground, the first of the paratroopers to arrive. He had not been able to orientate himself during his short drop, and after a soft landing he undid his harness, gathered himself together, looked around, and realised he did not know where he was. The church tower at Ranville was supposed to be his recognition point, but he was in a little depression in a corn field and could not see it. Nor could he see any of his men. He had set out to find them, especially his wireless operator, when he heard Brotheridge's Sten go off. That fixed his rendezvous point exactly in his mind and he began walking towards it, as fast as a man could move at night through a corn field. On the way he picked up one private.

Over England, at 0020, Captain Richard Todd's Stirling

bomber began to straighten out for its run over the Channel. Todd, twenty-four years old, had set aside a promising acting career to join the paratroopers. Commissioned early in 1941, he was in the 7th Battalion of the 5th Brigade of the 6th Airborne Division. The colonel of the battalion, Geoffrey Pine Coffin, was in the same group of Stirlings as Todd – they were on their way to reinforce the *coup de main* party at the bridge.

Todd was supposed to fly in Stirling no. 36, but as his stick jumped out of its truck and started to climb aboard the aircraft, a senior RAF officer stepped forward and said he was going along, and that this plane would be no. 1. Todd protested at this decision, 'because we had our plan worked out, our jumping plan, but you can't argue with somebody senior to you. I was lucky, in fact, because the first twenty or so aircraft got in with the help of surprise, and when I was down there looking up at the others streaming in, the numbers in the thirties were all getting knocked down. The one that replaced me was knocked down and all the chaps on it were lost, so I had a bit of luck that night.'

At 0020 hours, Fox and his platoon had an easy landing some 300 metres from the river bridge. According to Fox, the real leader in the platoon was Sergeant Thornton. 'In barracks he was a quiet, unobtrusive man who would as soon sweep the barrack room himself as order a soldier to do it. But in action he was absolutely first-class, and he virtually commanded the platoon. I was the figurehead and did more or less what he told me to do.'

When they landed, Thornton reminded Fox that he had forgotten to open the door; when Fox could not get it open, Thornton showed him how to do it. When they got out and formed up, a corporal was supposed to move off with the lead section, Fox following at the head of the other two sections. But the corporal just stood there. Fox approached him to ask what was the matter; the corporal replied that he could see someone with a machine-gun up ahead. 'To hell with it', responded Fox, 'let's get cracking'. But the corporal still would not move.

Fox started off himself and almost immediately there was a burst of fire from an enemy MG 34. Everyone hit the ground.

'Then', according to Fox, 'dear old Thornton had got from way back in his position a mortar going, and he put a mortar slap down, a fabulous shot, right on the machine-gun, so we just rushed the bridge, all the chaps yelling, "Fox, Fox, Fox Fox, Fox".'

They reached the east bank, Lieutenant Fox in the lead. There was no opposition – the sentries had run off when the mortar was fired. As Fox stood there, panting and drinking in his victory, Thornton came up to him. Thornton said he had set up the Bren gun on the inside of the bridge, so that he could cover the advance party. Then he suggested to Fox that it might be a good idea to spread out a bit, instead of standing all bunched together on the end of the bridge. Fox agreed and spread the men out.

At 0021, Sweeney's glider was almost on the ground. Sweeney called out, 'Good luck, lads. Don't forget that as soon as we land, we're out and no hesitating'. Then he heard the glider pilot say, 'Oh, damn it'. The Horsa had hit a slight air pocket and dropped to the ground sooner than the pilot wanted it to. The landing itself was smooth, but the pilot apologised. 'I'm sorry, I've landed about 400 yards short.' Actually, he was closer to 700 metres short.

After his platoon had left the glider, Sweeney gathered the men and set off at a trot. They could hear the battle going on for the canal bridge. Almost immediately he fell into a drainage ditch and was soaked, but got out again and started doubling forward. When the platoon reached the river bridge they charged across, shouting 'Easy, Easy, Easy', at the top of their lungs. Because there was no opposition, Sweeney half-suspected that either Priday's or Fox's platoon had got there before him, 'but I still had that awful feeling as I went over the bridge that the thing might blow up in our face'. He left one section at the west bank, crossing with the other two sections.

There, on the other side of the bridge, were Fox and his men, all shouting back 'Fox, Fox, Fox'. The calm of the scene came as something of a disappointment: 'we were all worked up to kill the enemy, bayonet the enemy, be blown up or something and then we see nothing more than the unmistakable figure of Dennis Fox'.

Sweeney had often seen Fox standing, just like that, during the practice runs back at Exeter. Fox's great concern on the runs, like that of all the platoon leaders, had always been the umpires and how they would rate his performance.

Sweeney raced up to Fox. 'Dennis, Dennis, how are you? Is everything all right?'

Fox looked him up and down. 'Yes, I think so, Tod', he replied. 'But I can't find the bloody umpires.'

By 0021, the three platoons at the canal bridge had subdued most resistance from the machine-gun pits and the slit trenches – the enemy had either been killed or run off. Men previously detailed for the job began moving into the bunkers. This was not the most pleasant of tasks, according to Sandy Smith: 'we were not taking any prisoners or messing around, we just threw phosphorus grenades down and high-explosive grenades into the dugouts there, and anything that moved we shot.'

Wally Parr and Charlie Gardner led the way into the bunkers on the left. When they were underground, Parr pulled open the door to the first bunker and threw in a grenade. Immediately after the explosion, Gardner stepped into the open door and sprayed the room with his Sten gun. Parr and Gardner repeated the process twice; then, having cleaned out that bunker, and with their ear-drums apparently shattered for ever by the concussion and the sound, they went back up to the ground.

Their next task was to meet with Brotheridge, whose command post was scheduled to be the café, and take up firing positions. As they rounded the corner of the café, Gardner threw a phosphorus grenade towards the sound of sporadic German small-arms fire. Parr shouted at him, 'Don't throw another one of those bloody things, we'll never see what's happening.'

Parr asked another member of his platoon, 'Where's Danny?' (To his face, the men all called him 'Mr Brotheridge' but they thought of him and referred to him as 'Danny'.)

'Where's Danny?' Parr repeated. The soldier did not know, and said that he had not seen Brotheridge since crossing the bridge. 'Well', Parr thought, 'he's here, Danny must be here somewhere'. Parr started to run around the café when he ran past a man lying opposite the café in the road. Parr glanced at him as he ran on. 'Hang on', he said to himself, and went back and knelt down. 'I looked at him, and it was Danny Brotheridge. His eyes were open and his lips moving. I put me hand under his head to lift him up. He just looked. His eyes sort of rolled back. He just choked and lay back. My hand was covered in blood.

'I just looked at him and thought, "My God, what a waste!" All the years of training we put in to do this job – it lasted only seconds." '

Jack Bailey came running up. 'What the hell's going on?' he asked Parr. 'It's Danny', Parr replied. 'He's had it'. 'Christ Almighty', Bailey muttered.

Sandy Smith, who had thought that everyone was going to be incredibly brave, was learning about war. He was astonished to see one of his best men, someone he had come to depend on heavily during exercises and who he thought would prove to be a real leader on the other side, cowering and praying in a slit trench. Another reported a sprained ankle from the crash and limped off to seek protection. He had not been limping earlier. Lieutenant Smith lost a lot of illusions very fast.

On the other side of the bridge, David Wood's platoon was clearing out the slit trenches and the bunkers on each side of the road. Shouting 'Baker, Baker, Baker' as they moved along, they shot at any sign of movement in the trenches. The task went quickly enough, most of the enemy having run away, and soon the trenches were pronounced clear. Wood discovered an intact MG 34 with a complete belt of ammunition on it, and detailed two of his men to take over the gun. The remainder filled in the trenches, and Wood went back to report to Howard that he had accomplished his mission. As he moved back, congratulating his platoon along the way, there was a burst from a Schmeisser. Three bullets hit virtually simultaneously in his left leg, and Wood went down, frightened, unable to move, bleeding profusely.

Wallwork, meanwhile, had come to, lying on his stomach under the glider. 'I was stuck. Ainsworth was stuck and I could hear him. I came round. Ainsworth seemed to be in bad shape and yet he would shout. All he could say was, "Jim, are you all right, Jim? Are you all right, Jimmy?" and he was a sight worse than I was, he was pinned under.'

Wallwork asked if Ainsworth could crawl out. No. Well, could he get out if the glider were picked up? Yes. 'And I lifted the thing. I felt like I was lifting the whole bloody glider, I felt like Hercules when I picked this thing up. Ainsworth managed to crawl out.' As a medic looked after Ainsworth, Wallwork began to unload ammunition from the glider and carry it forward to the fighting platoons. He did not yet realise that his head and forehead had been badly cut, and that blood was streaking down his face.

Over at the river bridge, Sweeney's section on the far bank heard a patrol coming up the towpath from the direction of Caen. The section leader challenged the patrol with the password, 'V'. But the answer from the patrol was certainly not 'for Victory', and it sounded like German. The entire section opened fire and killed all four men. Later investigation showed that among them was a gagged British para, one of the pathfinders who had been caught by the German patrol, and who was evidently being taken back to headquarters for interrogation.

By 0022, Howard had set up his command post in the trench on the northeast corner of the bridge. Corporal Tappenden, the wireless operator, was at his side. Howard tried to make out how the fire-fight was going at his bridge as he waited for reports from the river bridge. The first information to come to him was nearly devastating: Brotheridge was down.

'It really shook me', Howard says, 'because it was Den and how much of a friend he was, and because my leading platoon was now without an officer.' The next bit of news was just as bad: Wood, and his wireless operator and his sergeant, were all wounded and out of action. Another runner reported that Lieutenant Smith had about lost his wrist, and had a badly wrenched knee to boot.

All three platoon leaders gone, and in less than ten minutes! Fortunately, the sergeants were thoroughly familiar with the various tasks and could take over; in Wood's platoon, a corporal took charge. In addition, Smith was still on his feet, although hardly mobile and in great pain. Howard had no effective officers at the canal bridge, and did not know what was happening at the river bridge. Gloom might have given way to despair had he known that his second-in-command, Captain Priday, and one-sixth of his fighting strength, had landed twenty kilometres away on the River Dives.

Howard kept asking Tappenden if he had heard anything from nos. 4, 5, and 6. 'No', Tappenden kept replying, 'no, no'.

Over the next two minutes, there was a dramatic change in the nature of the reports coming in, and consequently in Howard's mood. First Jock Neilson of the sappers came up to him: 'There were no explosives under the bridge, John.' Neilson explained that the bridge had been prepared for demolition, but the explosives themselves had not been put into their chambers. The sappers removed all the firing mechanisms, then went into the line as infantry. The next day they found the explosives in a nearby shed.

Knowing that the bridge would not be blown was a great relief to Howard. Just as good, the firing was dying down, and from what Howard could see through all the smoke and in the on-again-off-again moonlight, his people had control of both ends of the canal bridge. Just as he realised that he had pulled off Ham, Tappenden tugged at his battle smock. Message coming in from Sweeney's platoon: 'We captured the bridge without firing a shot'.

Ham *and* Jam! D Company had done it. Howard felt a tremendous exultation, and a surge of pride in his company. 'Send it out', he told Tappenden. 'Ham and Jam, Ham and Jam, keep it up until you get an acknowledgement.' Tappenden began incessantly calling out, 'Ham and Jam, Ham and Jam'.

Tappenden was beaming the message towards the east, hoping that it would be picked up by Brigadier Poett. What he and Howard did not know was that Poett had never found his wireless operator, and was trudging towards them with only one soldier to accompany him.

Hold until relieved. Those were Howard's orders, but one Brigadier and one rifleman did not constitute much of a relief.

CHAPTER SIX

D-Day: 0026 to 0600 hours

With the bridges captured, Howard's concern shifted from the offence to the defence. He could expect a German counter-attack at any time. He was not concerned about the safety of the river bridge, because British paratroopers were scheduled to begin landing around Ranville within thirty minutes, and they could take care of protecting that bridge. But to the front of the canal bridge, towards the west, he had no help at all – and a countryside jammed with German troops, German tanks, German lorries. Howard sent a runner over to the river bridge, with orders for Fox to bring his platoon over to the canal bridge. When Fox arrived, Howard intended to push his platoon forward to the T junction, as the lead platoon. Howard wanted them to take a fighting patrol role, breaking up any enemy preparations for attack.

Howard knew that it would take Fox some time to call his men in from their firing positions, for Sweeney to take over, and for Fox to march the quarter-mile from one bridge to the other. But he could already hear tanks starting up in Le Port. They headed south along the road to Benouville. To Howard's immense relief, the tanks did not turn at the T junction and come down towards the bridge, but instead continued on into Benouville. He surmised that the commanders of the garrisons in the two villages were conferring. Howard knew that the tanks would be back.

Tanks coming down from the T junction were by far his greatest worry. With their machine-gun and cannon, German

84

tanks could easily drive D Company away from the bridges. To stop them he had only the Piat guns, one per platoon, and the Gammon bombs. Parr came back to the CP from the west end of the bridge to report that he had heard tanks, and to announce that he was going back to the glider for the Piat. 'Get cracking', Howard said.

Parr went down the embankment, climbed into the glider, and 'I couldn't see a bloody thing, could I? There was no torch, I started scrambling around and at last I found the Piat.' Parr picked it up, tripped over some ammunition, sprawled, got up again, and discovered the barrel of the Piat had bent. The gun was useless. Parr threw it down with disgust, grabbed some ammunition, and returned to the CP to tell Howard that the Piat was kaput.

Howard yelled across at one of Sandy Smith's men to make sure they had their Piat. Jim Wallwork trudged by, loaded like a pack horse, carrying ammunition up to the forward platoons. Howard looked at Wallwork's blood-covered face and thought, 'That's a strange colour of camouflage to be wearing at night'. He told Wallwork 'he looked like a bloody Red Indian'. Wallwork explained about his cuts – by this time, Wallwork thought he had lost his eye – and went about his business.

At about 0045, Dr Vaughan returned to consciousness. He pulled himself out of the mud and staggered back to the glider, where he could hear one of the pilots moaning. Unable to get the man out of the wreckage, he gave him a shot of morphine. Then Vaughan walked towards the bridge, where he could hear Tappenden calling out, 'Ham and Jam, Ham and Jam'.

Vaughan stumbled his way to the CP and found Howard 'sitting in this trench looking perfectly happy, issuing orders right and left'.

'Hello, Doc, how are you? Where the hell have you been?' Howard asked. Vaughan explained, and Howard told him to look after Brotheridge and Wood, who had been brought by stretcher to a little lane about 150 yards east of the bridge. (When Howard saw Brotheridge being carried past on the stretcher some minutes earlier, he could see that it was a fatal wound. 'At the top of my mind', Howard says, 'was the fact that

85

I knew that Margaret, his wife, was expecting a baby almost any time'.

Vaughan set off for the west end of the bridge. There were shrieks of 'Come back, Doc, come back, that's the wrong way!' Howard pointed him towards his destination, the first-aid post in the lane. Before letting the still badly confused Doc wander off again, Howard gave him a shot of whisky from his emergency flask.

Vaughan finally made it to the aid post, where he found Wood lying on his stretcher. He examined the splint the medical orderly had put on, found it good enough, and gave Wood a shot of morphine. Then he started staggering down the road, again in the wrong direction, again raising cries of 'Come back, wrong way, unfriendly!'

Returning to the aid post, Vaughan found Den Brotheridge. 'He was lying on his back looking up at the stars and looking terribly surprised, just surprised. And I found a bullet hole right in the middle of his neck.' Vaughan, recovering quickly from his daze, gave Brotheridge a shot of morphine and dressed his wound. Soon after that Brotheridge died, the first Allied soldier to be killed in action on D-Day.

All this time, Tappenden was calling out, 'Ham and Jam, Ham and Jam'. And as the Doc looked after Den and the several other casualties, Fox and his platoon came marching in, in good order. Howard told him, 'Number 5 task', and Fox began moving across the bridge. As he passed Smith he got a quick briefing – the tiny bridgehead was secure for the moment, but hostile fire was coming from houses in both Le Port and Benouville, and tanks had been heard.

Fox remarked that his Piat had been smashed in the landing. 'Take mine, old boy', Smith said, and handed his Piat to Fox. Fox in turn handed it to Sergeant Thornton. Poor Wagger Thornton, a man slightly smaller than average, was practically buried under equipment by now: he had on his pack, his grenade pouch, his Sten gun, magazines for the Bren gun and extra ammunition for himself. And now he was getting a Piat gun and two Piat bombs. Overloaded or not, he took the gun and followed Fox forward, towards the T junction.

At 0040, Richard Todd and his stick were over the Channel. Todd was standing over a hole in the bottom of the Stirling bomber, a leg on each side. On each leg he had a kit bag, one containing a rubber dinghy, the other entrenching tools. His Sten was strapped to his chest, and he carried a pack and a pouch full of grenades and plenty of extra ammunition. Todd's batman stood behind him, holding and trying to steady him as the Stirling took evasive action from the flak. 'Quite a lot of people did fall out over the sea from evasive action', according to Todd. His batman held tight to him, as the Channel slipped past below.

At precisely 0050, exactly on schedule, Howard heard low-flying bombers overhead, at about 400 feet. To the east and north of Ranville, flares – set by the pathfinders – began to light the sky. Simultaneously, German searchlights from every village in the area went on. Howard recalls the sight: 'We had a first-class view of the division coming in. Searchlights were lighting up the chutes and there was a bit of firing going on and you could see tracer bullets going up into the air as the paras floated down to the ground. It really was the most awe-inspiring sight. . . . Above all, it meant that we were no longer alone.'

Howard began blowing for all he was worth on his metal whistle, Dot, Dot, Dot (pause), Dash. It was his pre-arranged signal, V for Victory. Over and over he blew it, and the shrill sound carried for miles in the night air. This meant a great deal to the landing troops, says Howard. 'Paras who landed alone, in a tree or a bog, in a farmyard, alone, and away from their own friends, could hear that whistle. It not only meant that the bridges had been captured, but it also gave them an orientation.'

But it would take the paras at least an hour to get to the bridges in any significant numbers; meanwhile, the tanks were rumbling in Benouville. Wallwork, returning to his glider for another load, went by the CP 'and there was Howard, tooting on his bloody whistle and making all sorts of silly noises'. Howard stopped blowing long enough to tell Wallwork to get some Gammon bombs up to Fox and his men.

So, Wallwork says, it was 'Gammon bombs! Gammon

bombs! Bloody Gammon bombs! I bowled my flip line. I had already been to look for the damned things once and told Howard that there weren't any in the glider. But he said, "I saw those Gammon bombs on the glider. Get them!" so back I went panning through this rather badly broken glider looking for the flaming things'.

As Wallwork switched on his torch he heard a rat-tat-tat through the glider. A German in a trench down the canal had seen the light and turned his Schmeisser on the glider. 'So off went the light, and I thought, "Howard, you've had your bloody Gammon bombs".' Wallwork grabbed a load of ammunition and returned to the bridge, reporting to Howard on his way past that there were no Gammon bombs. (No one ever figured out what happened to them. Wallwork claims that Howard pitched them before take-off to lighten the load; Howard claims that they were pinched by the men from nos 2 and 3 platoons.)

Tappenden kept calling 'Ham and Jam'. Twice at least he really shouted it out, 'Ham and Jam, Ham and BLOODY Jam'.

At 0052 the target for Tappenden's message, Brigadier Poett, worked his way through the final few metres of corn and arrived at the river bridge. After checking with Sweeney on the situation there, he walked across to the canal bridge.

Howard's first thought, when he saw his brigadier coming towards him, was 'Sweeney's going to get a bloody rocket from me for not letting me know, either by runner or radio, that the brigadier was in the company area'. Meanwhile he gave his report, and Poett looked around. 'Well, everything seems all right, John', Poett said. They crossed the bridge and conferred with Smith. All three officers could hear the tanks and lorries in Benouville and Le Port; all three knew that if help did not arrive soon, they could lose their precarious hold on the bridge.

At 0052, Richard Todd landed, with other paras dropping all around him. Like Poett earlier, Todd could not get orientated because he could not see the steeple of the Ranville church. Tracer bullets were flying across the DZ, so he unbuckled and made for a nearby wood, where he hoped to meet other paras and get his bearings. He got them from Howard's whistle.

Major Nigel Taylor, commanding a company of the 7 Para Battalion, was also confused. The first man he ran into was an officer who had a bugler with him. The two had dropped earlier, with Poett and the pathfinders. Their job was to find the rendezvous in Ranville, then start blowing on the bugle the regimental call of the Somerset Light Infantry. But the officer told Taylor, 'I've been looking for this damned rendezvous for three-quarters of an hour, and I can't find it'. They ducked into a wood, where they found Colonel Pine Coffin, the battalion commander. He too was lost. They got out their maps, put a torch on them, but still could not make out their location. Then they, too, heard Howard's whistle.

Knowing where Howard was did not solve all Pine Coffin's problems. Fewer than 100 men of his more than 500-man force had gathered around him. He knew that Howard had the bridges, but as Nigel Taylor explains, he also knew that 'the Germans had a propensity for immediate counter-attack. Our job was to get down across that bridge, to the other side. We were the only battalion scheduled to go on that side, west of the canal. So Pine Coffin's dilemma was, should he move off with insufficient men to do the job, or wait for the battalion to form up. He knew he had to get off as quickly as possible to relieve John Howard.' At about 0110, Pine Coffin decided to set off at double-time for the bridges, leaving one man to direct the rest of his battalion when it came up.

In Ranville, meanwhile, Major Schmidt had decided he should investigate all the shooting going on at his bridges. He grabbed one last plateful of food, a bottle of wine, his girlfriend, and his driver, summoned his motorcycle escort, and roared off for the river bridge. He was in a big, open Mercedes. As they sped past his girlfriend's house, she screamed that she wanted to be let out. Schmidt ordered the driver to halt, opened the door for her, and sped on.

The Mercedes came on so fast that Sweeney's men did not have a chance to fire at it until it was already on the bridge. They did open up on the motorcycle that was trailing the car, hit it broadside, and sent it and its driver skidding off into the river. Sweeney, on the west bank, fired his Sten at the speeding

Mercedes, riddling it and causing it to run straight off the road. Sweeney's men picked up the driver and Major Schmidt, both badly wounded. In the car they found wine, plates of food, lipstick, stockings and lingerie. Sweeney had the wounded Schmidt and his driver put on stretchers and carried over to the first-aid post.

By the time he arrived at the post, Schmidt had recovered from his initial shock. He began screaming, in perfect English, that he was the commander of the garrison at the bridge, that he had let his Führer down, that he was humiliated and had lost his honour, and that he demanded to be shot. Alternatively he was yelling that 'You British are going to be thrown back, my Führer will see to that, you're going to be thrown back into the sea'.

Vaughan got out a syringe of morphine and jabbed Schmidt with it, then set about dressing his wounds. The effect of the morphine, Vaughan reports, 'was to induce him to take a more reasonable view of things and after ten minutes more of haranguing me about the futility of the Allied attempt to defeat the master race, he relaxed. Soon he was profusely thanking me for my medical attentions.' Howard confiscated Schmidt's binoculars.

Schmidt's driver, a sixteen-year-old German, had had one leg blown off. The other leg was just hanging – Vaughan removed it with his scissors. Within half an hour, the boy was dead.

By 0115, Howard had completed his defensive arrangements at the canal bridge. He had Wood's platoon with him at the east end along with the sappers, whom he had organised into a reserve platoon patrolling between the two bridges. On the west side, Brotheridge's platoon held the café and the ground around it, while Smith's platoon held the bunkers to the right. Smith was in command of both platoons, but he was growing increasingly groggy from loss of blood and the intense pain in his knee, which had started to stiffen. Fox was up ahead, towards the T junction, with Thornton carrying the only working Piat that side of the bridge. The paras of the 7th Battalion were on their way, but their arrival time – and their strength – was uncertain.

Howard could hear tanks. He was desperate to establish

radio communication with Fox, but could not. Then he saw a tank swing slowly, ever so slowly, down towards the bridge, its great cannon sniffing the air like the trunk of some prehistoric monster. 'And it wasn't long before we could see a couple of them about twenty-five yards apart moving very, very slowly. They obviously did not know what to expect when they got down to the bridges.'

Everything now hung in the balance. If the Germans retook the canal bridge, they would then drive on to overwhelm Sweeney's platoon at the river bridge. There they could have set up a defensive perimeter, bolstered by tanks, so strong that the 6th Airborne Division would have found it difficult, perhaps impossible, to break through. If that happened, the division would be isolated, without anti-tank weapons to fight off von Luck's armour.

In other words a great deal was at stake up there near the T junction. Fittingly, as so much was at stake, the battle at the bridge at 0130 on D-Day provided a fair test of the British and German armies of World War II. Each side had advantages and disadvantages. Howard's opponents were the company commanders in Benouville and Le Port. Like Howard, they had been training for over a year for this moment. They had been caught by surprise, but the troops at the bridge had been their worst troops, not much of a loss. In Benouville, the 1st Panzer Engineering Company of the 716 Infantry Division, and in Le Port the 2nd Engineers, were slightly better quality troops. The whole German military tradition, reinforced by their orders, compelled them to launch an immediate counter-attack. They had the platoons to do it with, and the armoured vehicles. What they did not have was a sure sense of the situation, because they kept getting conflicting reports.

Those conflicting reports were one of the weaknesses of the German army in France. They came about partly because of the language difficulties. The officers could not understand Polish or Russian, the men could not understand much German. The larger problem was the presence of so many conscripted foreigners in their companies, which in turn reflected Germany's most basic problem in World War II. Germany had badly overreached herself. Her population could not provide all the troops required on the various fronts. Filling the trenches along the Atlantic Wall with what amounted to slaves from East Europe looked good on paper, but in practice such soldiers were nearly worthless.

On the other hand, German industry did get steady production out of slave labour. Germany had been able to provide her troops with the best weapons in the world, and in abundance. By comparison, British industrial output was woefully inferior, both in quantity and quality (the British, of course, were far ahead of the Germans in aircraft and ship construction).

But although his arms were inferior, Howard was commanding British troops, and every man among them a volunteer who was superbly trained. They were vastly superior to their opponents. Except for Fox and the crippled Smith, Howard was without officers on the canal bridge, but he personally enjoyed one great advantage over the German commanders. He was in his element, in the middle of the night, fresh, alert, capable of making snap decisions, getting accurate reports from his equally fresh and alert men. The German commanders were confused, getting conflicting reports, tired and sleepy. Howard had placed his platoons exactly where he had planned to put them, with three on the west side to meet the first attacks, two in reserve on the east side (including the sappers) and one at the river bridge. Howard had seen to it that his anti-tank capability was exactly where he had planned to put it, up near the T junction. The German commanders, by way of contrast, were groping, hardly sure of where their own platoons were, unable to decide what to do.

The problem was, how could Howard's men deal with those tanks? They could not find their Gammon bombs, and hand-thrown grenades were of little or no use because they usually bounced off the tank and exploded harmlessly in the air. Bren and Sten guns were absolutely useless. The only weapon Howard had to stop those tanks with was Sergeant Thornton's Piat gun.

That gun, and the fact that he had trained D Company for precisely this moment, the first contact with tanks. Howard felt confident that Thornton was at the top of his form, totally alert, not the least bothered by the darkness or the hour. And Thornton was fully proficient in the use of a Piat: he knew precisely where he should hit the lead tank to knock it out.

Others were not quite so confident. Sandy Smith recalls 'hearing this bloody thing, feeling a sense of absolute terror, saying my God, what the hell am I going to do with these tanks coming down the road?' Billy Gray, who had taken up a position in an unoccupied German gun pit, saw the tank coming down the road and thought, 'that was it, we would never stop a tank. It was about twenty yards away from us, because we were up on this little hillock but it did give a sort of field of fire straight up the road. We fired up the road at anything we could see moving.'

Gray was tempted to fire at the tank, as most men in their first hour of combat would have done. But they had been trained not to fire; and they did what their training dictated. They did not, in short, reveal their positions, thus luring the tank into the killing area.

Howard had expected the tanks to be preceded by an infantry reconnaissance patrol – that was the way he would have done it – but the Germans had neglected to do so. Their infantry platoons were following the two tanks. So the tanks rolled forward, ever so slowly, the tank crews unaware that they had already crossed the front line.

The first Allied company in the invasion was about to meet the first German counter-attack. It all came down to Thornton, and the German tank crews. Their visibility was such that they could not see Thornton, half-buried as he was under that pile of equipment. Thornton was about thirty yards from the T junction, and he willingly admits that 'I was shaking like a bloody leaf!' With the sound of the tank coming towards him, he fingered his Piat.

Thornton's confidence in the gun was low, given its effective range of about fifty yards.

You're a dead loss if you try to go further. Even fifty yards is stretching it, especially at night. Another thing is that you must never, never miss. If you do you've had it because by the time you reload the thing and cock it, which is a bloody

93

chore on its own, everything's gone, you're done. It's drilled into your brain that you mustn't miss.

Thornton wanted to shoot at the shortest possible distance.

And sure enough, in about three minutes, this bloody great thing appears. I was more hearing it than seeing it, in the dark, it was rattling away there, and it turned out to be a Mark IV tank coming along pretty slowly, and they hung around for a few seconds to figure out where they were and what was happening ahead. Only had two of the bombs with me. Told myself you mustn't miss. Anyhow, although I was shaking, I took an aim and bang, off it went.

The tank had just turned at the T junction.

I hit him round about right bang in the middle. I made sure I had him right in the middle. I was so excited and so shaking I had to move back a bit.

Then all hell broke loose. The explosion from the Piat bomb penetrated the tank, setting off the machine-gun clips, which started setting off grenades, which started setting off shells. Everyone who saw the tank hit testifies to the absolute brilliance, the magnificence, of the fireworks that followed. As Glen Gray points out in his book *The Warriors*, a battlefield can be an extraordinary visual display, with red, green, or orange tracers skimming about, explosions going off here and there, flares lighting up portions of the sky. But few warriors have ever seen such a display as that near Benouville bridge before dawn on D-Day.

The din, the light show, could be heard and seen by paratroopers many kilometres from the bridge. Indeed, it provided an orientation and thus got them moving in the right direction.

When the tank went off, Fox took protection behind a wall. He explains:

You couldn't go very far because, whiz-bang, a bullet or shell went straight past you. But finally it died down and incredibly we heard this man crying out. Old Tommy Clare couldn't stand it any longer and he went straight out up to the tank and it was blazing away and he found the driver had got out of the tank and was lying beside it still conscious. Both legs were gone, he had been hit in the knees getting out. Clare was always kind, and an immensely strong fellow (back in barracks he once broke a man's jaws by just one blow). He hunched this poor old German on his back and took him to the first-aid post. I thought it was useless of course, but, in fact, I believe the man lived.

He did, but only for a few more hours. He turned out to be the commander of the 1st Panzer Engineering Company.

The fireworks show went on and on – altogether it lasted for more than an hour – and it helped convince the German company commanders that the British were present in great strength. Indeed, the lieutenant in the second tank withdrew to Benouville, where he reported that the British had six-pounder anti-tank guns at the bridge. The German officers decided that they would have to wait until dawn and a clarification of the situation before launching another counter-attack. Meanwhile, the lead tank smouldered, blocking the enemy's movements towards the bridge. John Howard's men had won the battle of the night.

By the time the tank went up, at about 0130 hours, Poett's men of the 5th Para Brigade, led by Pine Coffin's 7th Battalion, with Nigel Taylor's company leading the way, were double-timing towards the bridge – at less than one-third of their full strength. The paras knew they were late, and they thought from the fireworks that Howard was undergoing intensive attacks. But, as Taylor explains, 'it's very difficult to double in the dark carrying a heavy weight on uneven ground'.

When they got on the road leading to the bridges, they ran into Brigadier Poett, who was headed back towards his CP in Ranville. 'Come on Nigel', Poett called out to Taylor in his high-pitched voice. 'Double, double, double.' Taylor thought the order rather superfluous, but in fact his men did break into 'a rather shambling run'.

Richard Todd was in the group. He recalls the paratrooper medical officer catching up with him, grabbing him by the arm, and saying, 'Can I come with you? You see I'm not used to this sort of thing.' The doctor 'was rather horrified because we passed a German who had had his head shot off, but his arms and legs were still waving about and strange noises were coming out of him, and I thought even the doctor was a bit turned over by that'.

Todd remembers thinking, as he was running between the river and the canal bridges, 'Now we're really going into it, because there was a hell of an explosion and a terrific amount of firing, and tracers going in all directions. It looked like there was a real fight going on.' Major Taylor thought, 'Oh, Lord, I'm going to have to commit my company straight into battle on the trot'.

When 7th Battalion arrived at the bridge, Howard gave the leaders a quick briefing. The paras then went across, Nigel Taylor's company moving out to the left, into Benouville, while the other companies moved right, into Le Port. Richard Todd took up his position on a knoll just below the little church in Le Port, while Taylor led his company to prearranged platoon positions in Benouville, cutting the main road from Caen to the coast at Ouistreham. Taylor recalls that, except for the tank exploding in the background, within the hour 'everything was absolutely dead quiet'. The Germans had settled down to await the outcome of the 'battle' at the T junction.

A German motorcycle started up and the driver came around the corner, headed for the T junction. Taylor's men were on both sides of the road, 'and they've been training for God knows how many years to kill Germans, and this is the first one they've seen'. They all opened up. As the driver went into shock from the impact of a half-dozen or more bullets, his big twin-engined BMW bike flipped over and came down on him. The throttle was stuck on full, and the bike was in gear. 'It was absolutely roaring its head off, and every time it hit the ground the thing was bucking, shying about.' The bike struck one of Taylor's men, causing injuries that later resulted in death, before someone finally got the engine shut off. It was about 0230 hours.

At 0300 hours, Howard got a radio message from Sweeney, saying that Pine Coffin and his battalion headquarters were crossing the river bridge, headed towards the canal. Howard immediately started walking east, and met Pine Coffin half-way between the bridges. They walked back to the canal together, Howard telling Pine Coffin what had happened and what the situation was, so that by the time they arrived at the canal bridge Pine Coffin was already in the picture.

As he crossed the bridge, Pine Coffin queried Sergeant Thornton. Nodding towards the burning tank, the colonel asked, 'What the bloody hell's going on up there?'

'It's only a bloody old tank going off', Thornton replied, 'but it is making an awful racket'.

Pine Coffin grinned. 'I should say so.' Then he turned right, to make his headquarters on an embankment facing the canal, right on the edge of Le Port near the church. Howard followed soon afterwards to attend an 'O' group meeting called by Pine Coffin. Returning to the bridge, Howard reconnoitred lines of approach and likely counter-attack areas. While he did so he became mixed up in fighting going on between 7 Para and the enemy, and only vigorous swearing prevented him being shot by a para corporal.

After unloading the Horsa he had flown in as no. 2 glider pilot, Sergeant Boland went off exploring. He headed south, walking beside and below the tow path, and got to the outskirts of Caen. His may have been the deepest penetration of D-Day, although as Boland points out, there were scattered British paras dropping all around him, and some of the paras possibly came down even closer to Caen. At any event, it would be some weeks later before British and Canadian forces got that far again.

Boland says 'I decided I had better go back because it was bloody dangerous, not from the Germans but from bloody paras who were a bit trigger-happy. They'd landed all over the place, up trees, God knows where, and were very susceptible to firing at anybody coming from that direction.' After establishing his identity by using the password, Boland led a group of paras back to the bridge.

When he arrived, he saw Wallwork sitting on the bank. 'How

are you, Jim?' he asked. Wallwork looked past Boland, saw the paras, and went into a rocket. 'Where have you been till now?' he demanded. 'We'd all thought you were on a forty-eight-hour pass. The bloody war is over.'

'The paras thought they were rescuing us', Boland says. 'We felt we were rescuing them.'

The arrival of the 7th Battalion freed D Company from its patrolling responsibilities on the west bank and allowed Howard to pull his men back to the ground between the two bridges, where they were held as a reserve company.

When Wally Parr arrived, he set to examining the anti-tank gun emplacement, which had been unmanned when the British arrived and practically unnoticed since. Parr discovered a labyrinth of tunnels under the emplacement, and began exploring with the aid of another private. He discovered sleeping quarters. There was nothing in the first two compartments he checked, but in the third he found a man in bed, shaking violently. Parr slowly pulled back the blanket. 'There was this young soldier lying there in full uniform and he was shaking from top to toe.' Parr got him up with his bayonet, then took him up onto the ground and put him in the temporary POW cage. Then he returned to the gun pit, where he was joined by Billy Gray, Charlie Gardner, and Jack Bailey.

On his side of the bridge, across the road, Sergeant Thornton had persuaded Lieutenant Fox that there were indeed Germans still sleeping deep down in the dugouts. They set off together, with a torch, to find them. Thornton took Fox to a rear bunkroom, opened the door, and shone his light on three Germans, all snoring, with their rifles neatly stacked in the corner. Thornton removed the rifles, then covered Fox with his Sten while Fox shook the German in the top bunk. He snored on. Fox ripped off the blanket, shone his torch in the man's face, and told him to get up.

The German took a long look at Fox. He saw a wild-eyed young man, dressed in a ridiculous camouflage smock, his face blackened, pointing a little toy gun at him. He concluded that one of his buddies was playing a small joke. He told Fox, in German, but in a tone of voice and with a gesture that required no translation, to bugger off. Then he turned over and went back to sleep.

'It took the wind right out of my sails', Fox admits. 'Here I was a young officer, first bit of action, first German I had seen close up and giving him an order and receiving such a devastating response, well it was a bit deflating.' Thornton, meanwhile, laughed so hard he was crying. He collapsed on the floor, roaring with laughter.

Fox looked at him. 'To Hell with this', the lieutenant said to the sergeant. 'You take over.'

Fox went back up to ground level. Shortly thereafter, Thornton brought him a prisoner who spoke a bit of English. Thornton suggested that Fox might like to interrogate him. Fox began asking him about his unit, where other soldiers were located, and so on. But the German ignored his questions. Instead, he demanded to know, 'Who are you? What are you doing here? What is going on?'

Fox tried to explain that he was a British officer and that the German was a prisoner. The German could not believe it. 'Oh, come on, you don't mean it, you can't, well how did you land, we didn't hear you land, I mean where did you come from?' Poor Fox suddenly realised that he was the one being interrogated, and turned the proceedings back over to Thornton, but not before admiring photographs of the prisoner's family.

Von Luck was furious. At 0130 hours he received the first reports of British paratroopers in his area and immediately put his regiment on full alert. Locally he counted on his company commanders to launch their own counter-attacks wherever the British had captured a position, but the bulk of the regiment he ordered to assemble northeast of Caen. The assembly went smoothly enough, and by 0300 von Luck had gathered his men and their tanks and their SPVs, altogether an impressive force. The officers and men were standing beside their tanks and vehicles, engines running, ready to go.

But although von Luck had prepared for exactly this moment – knew where he wanted to go, in what strength, over what routes, with what alternatives – he could not give the order to go. Because of the jealousies and complexities of the German high command, because Rommel disagreed with Rundstedt, because Hitler was contemptuous of his generals and did not trust them to boot, the German command structure was a hopeless muddle. Without going into the details of such chaos, it is sufficient to note here that Hitler had retained personal control of the armoured divisions. They could not be used in a counter-attack until he had personally satisfied himself that the action was the real invasion. But Hitler was sleeping, and no one ever liked to wake him, and besides the reports coming into the German headquarters were confused and contradictory, and in any case hardly alarming enough to suggest that this was the main invasion. A night-time paratrooper drop might just be a diversion. So no order came to von Luck to move out.

> 'My idea, after I got more information about the parachute landings, and the gliders, was that a night attack would be the right way to counter-attack, starting at 3 or 4 in the morning, before the British could organise their defences, before their air force people could come, before the British navy could hit us. We were quite familiar with the ground and I think that we could have been able to get through to the bridge. The ultimate goal would be to cut off Howard's men from the main body of the landings. Then the whole situation on the east side of the bridge would have been different. The paratroopers would have been isolated and I would have communications with the other half of the 21st Panzer Division.'

But von Luck could not act on his own initiative, so there he sat. He was a senior officer in an army that prided itself on its ability to counter-attack, and leading one of the divisions Rommel most counted upon to lead the D-Day counter-attack. Personally quite certain of what he could accomplish, he had his attack routes all laid out. Yet he was rendered immobile by the intricacies of the leadership principle in the Third Reich.

Towards dawn, as von Luck waited impatiently, his men brought him two prisoners and a motorcycle. The prisoners were glider-borne troops who had come in with the first wave of 6th Airborne, east of Ranville. A German patrol had captured these two, and taken the motorcycle from the wrecked glider. Von Luck looked at the motorcycle. To his amazement, it was his. He had used it in North Africa in 1942 and lost it to the British in Tunisia in 1943; the British had brought the bike back to England, then brought it over to the Continent for the invasion. So von Luck got his bike back, and he used it till the end of the war. But he still could not move out.

The Gondrées, too, were immobilised in the cellar of their café. Thérèse, shivering in her nightdress, urged Georges to return to the ground floor and investigate. 'I am not a brave man', he later admitted, 'and I did not want to be shot, so I went upstairs on all fours and crawled to the first-floor window. There I heard talk outside but could not distinguish the words, so I pushed open the window and peeped out cautiously. I saw in front of the café two soldiers sitting near my petrol pump with a corpse between them.'

Georges was seen by one of the paras. 'Vous civile?' the soldier kept asking. Georges tried to assure him that he was indeed a civilian, but the man did not speak French and Georges, not knowing what was going on, did not want to reveal that he spoke English. He tried some halting German, that got nowhere, and he returned to the cellar, to await daylight and developments. Meanwhile Howard's men dug trenches in his garden.

By about 0500, Sandy Smith's knee had stiffened to the point of near-helplessness, his arm had swollen to more than twice normal size, his wrist was throbbing with pain. He approached Howard and said he thought he ought to go over to the first-aid post and have his wounds and injuries looked after. 'Must you go?' asked Howard, plaintively. Smith promised that he would be back in a minute. When he got to the post, Vaughan wanted to give him morphine. Smith refused. Vaughan said he could not go back to duty anyway, because he would be more of a nuisance than a help. Smith took the morphine.

Thus when Howard, returned from his hectic reconnaissance expedition, called for a meeting of platoon leaders at his CP, just before dawn, the full weight of the officer loss he had suffered struck him directly. Brotheridge's platoon (no. 1) was being commanded by Corporal Caine, the sergeant out of action and the lieutenant dead. Both Wood's and Smith's platoons (nos. 2 and 3) were also commanded by corporals. The second-in-command, Brian Priday, and the no. 4 platoon leader, Tony Hooper, had not been heard from. Only nos. 5 and 6 (led by Sweeney and Fox) had their full complement of officers and NCOs. There had been a dozen casualties, plus two dead.

Howard had not called his platoon leaders together to congratulate them on their accomplishment, but rather to prepare for the future. He went through various counter-attack routes and possibilities with them, in case the Germans broke through the lines of the 7 Para. Then he told them to have everyone stand-to until first light. At dawn, half the men could stand down and try to catch some sleep.

As the sky began to brighten, the light revealed D Company in occupation of the ground between the two bridges. It had carried out its mission.

The Germans wanted the bridge back, but their muddled command structure was hurting them badly. At 0300, von Luck had ordered the 8th Heavy Grenadier Battalion, which was one of his forward units located north of Caen and on the west side of the Orne waterways, to march on Benouville and retake the bridge. But, as Lieutenant Werner Kortenhaus reports, despite its name the 8th Heavy Grenadier Battalion had with it only its automatic weapons, some light anti-aircraft guns, and some grenade launches. No armour. Nevertheless, the Grenadiers attacked, inflicting casualties on Major Taylor's company and driving it back into the middle of Benouville. The Grenadiers then dug in around the Château and waited for the arrival of panzers from 21st Panzer Division.

Lieutenant Kortenhaus, who stood beside his tank, engine running, recalls his overwhelming thought over the last two hours of darkness: Why didn't the order to move come? If we had immediately marched we would have advanced under cover of darkness. But Hitler was still sleeping, and the order did not come.

CHAPTER SEVEN

D-Day: *0600 to 1200 hours*

Georges Gondrée, in his cellar, welcomed 'the wonderful air of dawn coming up over the land'. Through a hole in the cellar he could see figures moving about. 'I could hear no guttural orders, which I always associated with a German working-party', Gondrée later wrote, so he asked Thérèse to listen to the soldiers talk and determine whether they were speaking German or not. She did so and presently reported that she could not understand what they were saying. Then Georges listened again, 'and my heart began to beat quicker for I thought I heard the words "all right".'

Members of the 7th Battalion began knocking at the door. Gondrée decided to go up and open it before it was battered down. He admitted two men in battle smocks, with smoking Sten guns and coal-black faces. They asked, in French, whether there were any Germans in the house. He replied that there were not, took them into the bar and thence, with some reluctance on their part, which he overcame with smiles and body language, to the cellar. There he pointed to his wife and two children.

'For a moment there was silence. Then one soldier turned to the other and said, "It's all right, chum". At last I knew that they were English and burst into tears.' Thérèse began hugging and kissing the paratroopers, laughing and crying at the same time. As she kissed all the later arrivals, too, by mid-day her face was completely black. Howard remembers that 'she remained like that for two or three days afterwards, refusing to clear it off, telling everybody that this was from the British soldiers and she was terribly proud of it'.

Forty years later, Madame Gondrée remains the number-one fan of the British 6th Airborne Division. No man who was there on D-Day has ever had to pay for a drink at her café since, and many of the participants have been back often. The Gondrées were the first family to be liberated in France, and they have been generous in expressing their gratitude.

Free drinks for the British airborne chaps began immediately upon liberation, as Georges went out into his garden and dug up 98 bottles of champagne that he had buried in June 1940, just before the Germans arrived. Howard describes the scene: 'There was a helluva lot of cork-popping went on, enough so that it was heard on the other side of the canal'. Howard was on the café side of the bridge, consulting with Pine Coffin. The café had by then been turned into the regimental aid post. So, Howard says, 'by the time I got back to D Company I was told that everybody wanted to report sick. We stopped that lark, of course.' Then Howard confesses, 'Well, I didn't go back until I had had a sip, of course, of this wonderful champagne'. A bit embarrassed, he explains: 'It really was something to celebrate'.

Shortly after dawn, the seaborne invasion began. The largest armada ever assembled, nearly 6,000 ships of all types, lay off the Norman coast. As the big guns from the warships pounded the beaches, landing craft moved forward towards the coastline, carrying the first of the 127,000 soldiers who would cross the beach that day. Overhead, the largest air force ever assembled, nearly 5,000 planes, provided cover. It was a truly awesome display of the productivity of American, British and Canadian factories, its like probably never to be seen again. Ten years later, when he was President of the United States, Eisenhower said that another Overlord was impossible, because such a buildup of military strength on such a narrow front would be far too risky in the nuclear age – one or two atomic bombs would have wiped out the entire force.

The invasion stretched for some sixty miles, from Sword Beach on the left to Utah Beach on the right. German resistance was spotty, almost nonexistent at Utah Beach, quite effective and indeed almost decisive at Omaha Beach, determined but not irresistible at the British and Canadian beaches, where unusually high tides compressed the landings into narrow strips and added greatly to the problems of German artillery and small-arms fire. Whatever the problems, the invading forces overcame the initial opposition, and made a firm lodgement everywhere except at Omaha. On the far left, in the fighting closest to Howard and D Company, a bitter battle was underway in Ouistreham. Progress towards Caen was delayed.

Howard describes the landings from D Company's point of view:

The barrage coming in was quite terrific. It was as though you could feel the whole of the ground shaking towards the coast, and this was going on like Hell. Soon afterwards it seemed to get nearer. Well, they were obviously lifting the barrage further inland as our boats and craft came in, and it was very easy standing there and hearing all this going on and seeing all the smoke over in that direction, to realise what exactly was happening and keeping our fingers crossed for those poor buggers coming by sea. I was very pleased to be where I was, not with the seaborne chaps.

He quickly stopped indulging in sympathy for his seaborne comrades, because with full light sniper activity picked up dramatically, and movement over the bridge became highly dangerous. The general direction of the fire was from the west bank, towards Caen, where there was a heavily-wooded area and two dominant buildings, the château that was used as a maternity hospital, and the water tower. Where any specific sniper was located, D Company could not tell. But the snipers had the bridge under a tight control, if not a complete grip, and they were beginning to fire on the first-aid post, in its trench beside the road, where Vaughan and his aides were wearing Red Cross bands and obviously tending wounded.

David Wood, who was laying on a stretcher, three bullets in his leg, recalls that the first sniper bullet struck the ground near him and he thought he was going to be hit next. 'Then a shot which was far too close for comfort thudded into the ground right next to my head, and I looked up to see that my medical orderly had drawn his pistol to protect his patient, and had accidentally discharged it and very nearly finished me off.'

Smith was having his wrist bandaged by another orderly. He tells of how the orderly stood up and was shot 'straight through the chest, knocked absolutely miles backwards. He went hurtling across the road and landed on his back, screaming, "take my grenades out, take my grenades out". He was frightened of being shot again, with grenades in his pouches.' Someone got the grenades out, and he survived, but Smith remembers the incident as 'a very low point in my life. I remember also, I thought the next bullet was going to come for me. I felt terrible.' Vaughan, bending over a patient, looked up in the direction of the sniper, shook his fist, and declared, 'This isn't cricket'.

Later that morning, Wood and Smith were evacuated to a divisional aid post in Ranville, where they were also shot at and had to be moved again.

Parr, Gardner, Gray, and Bailey were in the gun pit, trying to figure out how the anti-tank gun worked. Howard had trained them on German small-arms, mortars, machine guns, and grenades, but not on artillery. 'We started figuring it out', Parr recalls, 'and we got the breech out, all the ammo you want downstairs, brought one shell up, put it in, closed the breech. Now', they wondered, 'how do you fire it?'

The four soldiers were standing in the gun pit. Because of its roof, the snipers could not get at them. They talked it over, trying to locate the firing mechanism. Finally Gardner asked, 'What's this?', and pressed a push button. 'There was the biggest explosion, the shell screamed off in the general direction of Caen and, of course, the case shot out of the back and if anybody had stood there it would have caved their ribs in. That's how we learned to fire the gun.'

After that, Parr gleefully admits, 'I had the time of my life firing that gun'. He and his mates were certain that the sniping was coming from the roof of the château. Parr began putting shells through the top floor of the building, spacing them along.

106

There was no discernible decrease in the volume of sniper fire, however, and the location of the snipers remained a mystery. In any case, the snipers were very good shots and highly professional soldiers.

Parr kept shooting, but Jack Bailey tired of the sport and went below, to brew up his first cup of tea of the day. Every time Parr fired, the chamber filled with dust, smoke, and loose sand came shaking down. Bailey called up, 'Now, Wally, no firing now, just give me three minutes'. Bailey took out his Tommy cooker, lit it, watched as the water came to a boil, shivered with pleasure as he thought how good that tea was going to taste, had his sugar ready to pop into it, when suddenly, 'Blam'. Wally had fired again. Dust, soot, and sand filled Bailey's mug of tea, and his Tommy cooker was out.

Bailey, certain Wally had timed it deliberately, came tearing up, looking – according to Parr – 'like a bloody lunatic'. Bailey threatened Parr with immediate dismemberment, but at heart Bailey is a gentle man, and by keeping the gun between himself and Bailey, Parr survived.

Howard dashed across the road, bending low, to find out what Parr was doing. When he realised that Parr was shooting at the château, he was horrified. Howard ordered Parr to cease fire immediately, then explained to him that the château was a maternity hospital. Parr says today, with a touch of chagrin, 'that was the first and only time I've ever shelled pregnant women and newborn babies'. After the war, reading a magazine article on German atrocities in occupied Europe, Parr came across a prime example: it seemed, according to the article, that before withdrawing from Benouville, the Germans had decided to give the village a lesson and methodically shelled the maternity hospital and ancient château!

Howard never did convince Parr that the Germans were not using the roof for sniping. As Howard returned to his CP, he called out, 'Now you keep that bloody so-and-so quiet, Parr, just keep it quiet. Only fire when necessary, and that doesn't mean at imaginary snipers.'

Soon Parr was shooting into the trees. Howard yelled, 'For Christ's sake, Parr, will you shut up! Keep that bloody gun quiet! I can't think over it.' Parr thought to himself, 'Nobody told me it was going to be a quiet war'. But he and his mates stopped firing and started cleaning up the shell casings scattered through the gun pit. It had suddenly occurred to them that if someone slipped on a case while he was carrying a shell, and if the shell fell point downwards into the brim-full ammunition room, they and their gun and the bridge itself would all go sky high.

By 0700, the British 3rd Division was landing at Sword Beach, and the big naval gunfire had lifted to start pounding both Caen and behind the beaches, en route passing over D Company's position. 'They sounded so big', Howard says, 'and being poor bloody infantry, we had never been under naval fire before and these damn great shells came sailing over, such a size that you automatically ducked, even in the pillbox, as one went over and my radio operator was standing next to me, very perturbed about this and finally Corporal Tappenden said, "Blimey, sir, they're firing jeeps".'

Someone brought in two prisoners, described by Howard as 'miserable little men, in civilian clothes, scantily dressed, very hungry'. They turned out to be Italians, slave labourers in the Todt Organization. Long, complicated sign-language communication finally revealed that they were the labourers designated to put the anti-glider poles in place. They had been doing their job, on Wallwork's LZ, and appeared quite harmless to Howard. He gave them some dry biscuits from his forty-eight-hour ration pack, then let them loose. The Italians, Howard relates, 'immediately went off towards the LZ where they proceeded in putting up the poles. You can just imagine the laughter that was caused all the way around to see these silly buggers putting up the poles.'

More questioning then revealed that the Italians were under the strictest orders to have those poles in the ground by twilight, June 6. They were sure the Germans would be back to check on their work, and if it were not done, 'they were in for the bloody high jump, so they'd better get on with it, and surrounded by our laughter, they got on with it, putting in the poles'.

At about 0800, Spitfires flew over, very high, at 6,000 or

7,000 feet. Howard put out ground-to-air signals, using silk scarves and parachutes spread over the ground, that meant, 'We're in charge here and everything's all right'. Three Spitfires – wearing, like all the other Allied aircraft that participated in the invasion, three white bars on each wing – peeled off, dived to 1,000 feet, circled the bridges doing victory roll after victory roll.

As they pulled away, one of them dropped an object. Howard thought the pilot had jettisoned his reserve petrol tank, but he sent a reconnaissance patrol to find out what it was. The patrol came back, 'and to our great surprise and amusement, it was the early editions from Fleet St. There was a scramble for them amongst all the troops, especially for the *Daily Mirror*, which had a cartoon strip called "Jane", and they were all scuffling for Jane. There were one or two moans about there being no mention of the invasion or of D Company at all.'

Throughout the morning, all movement in D Company's area was done crouched over, at a full sprint. Then, shortly after 0900, Howard experienced

. . . the wonderful sight of three tall figures walking down the road. Now, between the bridges you were generally out of line of the snipers, because of the trees along this side of the canal, and these three tall figures came marching down very smartly and they turned out to be General Gale, about six foot five inches, flanked by two six-foot brigadiers – Kindersley on one side, our own Air Landing Brigade commander, and Nigel Poett, commanding the 5th Para Brigade, on the other. And it really was a wonderful sight because they were turned out very, very smartly, wearing berets and in battle dress, and marching in step down the road. Richard Todd said that 'for sheer bravado and bravery it was one of the most memorable sights I've ever seen', and all the other men agreed.

Gale had come down by glider, about 0300, and established his headquarters in Ranville. He and his brigadiers were on their way to consult with Pine Coffin, whose 7th Battalion was hotly engaged with enemy patrols in Benouville and Le Port. Gale called out to D Company, as he marched along, 'Good show, chaps'. After a briefing from Howard, Gale and his companions marched across the bridge. They were shot at but not hit, and they never flinched.

As they disappeared into Pine Coffin's headquarters, two gun-boats suddenly appeared, coming up from the coast headed towards Caen. They were coming from the small harbour in Ouistreham, which was under attack by elements of Lord Lovat's Commando brigade. The gun-boats were obviously aware that the bridge was in unfriendly hands, because the lead boat came on at a steady speed, firing its 20mm cannon at the bridge. Parr could not shoot back with the anti-tank gun because the bridge and its superstructure blocked his field of fire. Corporal Godbold, commanding no. 2 platoon, was on the bank with a Piat. Howard ordered his men to hold their fire until the gun-boat was in Godbold's range. Then some of 7 Para on the other side started firing at the boat. Godbold let go, at maximum range, and to his amazement he saw the Piat bomb explode inside the wheelhouse. The gunboat turned sideways, the bow plunged into the para bank, the stern jammed against D Company's side.

Germans started running off the stern, hands high, shouting 'Kamerad, Kamerad'. The captain, dazed but defiant, had to be forced off the boat. Howard remembers him as being eighteen or nineteen; very tall, and speaking good English. 'He was ranting on in English about what a stupid thing it was for us to think of invading the continent, and when his Führer got to hear about it we would be driven back into the sea. He was making the most insulting remarks and I had the greatest difficulty stopping my chaps from getting hold and lynching that bastard on the spot.' But Howard knew that intelligence would want to see the young officer immediately, so he had the prisoner marched off towards the POW cage in Ranville. 'And he had to be frog-marched back because he was so truculent and shouting away all through the time.'

The sappers looked around the boat, examining equipment, searching for ammunition and guns. One of them, a 19-year-old named Ramsey, found a bottle of brandy and stuck it in his battle smock. His commander, Jock Neilson, noticed the bulge and asked what it was. The sapper showed him and Neilson took it, saying, 'You are not old enough for that'. The sapper complains, 'I never saw a drop of that bloody brandy'.

Near Caen, von Luck was close to despair. The naval bombardment raining down on Caen was the most tremendous he had seen in all his years at war. Although his assembly point was camouflaged and so far untouched, he knew that when he started to move – when he finally got the order to go – he would be spotted immediately by the Allied reconnaissance aircraft overhead, his position reported to the big ships out in the Channel, and a torrent of shells would come down on his head.

Under the circumstances, he doubted that he could get through the 6th Airborne and recapture the bridges. His superiors agreed with him, and they decided that they would destroy the bridges and thus isolate the 6th Airborne. They began to organise a gun-boat packed with infantry, meanwhile sending out frogmen and a fighter-bomber from Caen to destroy the bridge.

At about 1000, the German fighter-bomber came flying directly out of the sun, over the river bridge, skimming along just above the trees lining the road, obviously headed for the canal bridge. Howard dived into his pillbox; his men dived into trenches. They poked their heads out to watch as the pilot dropped his bomb. It was a direct hit on the bridge tower, but it did not explode. Instead it clanged onto the bridge and then dropped into the canal. It was a dud.

Howard comments, 'What a bit of luck that was . . . and what a wonderful shot by that German pilot'. The dent is there on the bridge to this day.

The two frogmen were easily disposed of by riflemen along the banks of the canal. On the ground, however, the Germans were pushing the British back. Nigel Taylor's was the only company of 7th Battalion in Benouville. It was desperately understrength and very hard pressed by the increasingly powerful German counter-attacks. The two companies in Le Port were similarly situated and, like Taylor, were having to give up some ground.

As the Germans moved forward, they began putting some of

111

their SPVs into action. These vehicles belonged to von Luck's regiment, but were attached to forward companies that were expected to act on their own initiative rather than report back to the regimental assembly area. The British called the rocket launchers on the SPVs 'Moaning Minnies'. What they remember most about them, Howard says, 'apart from the frightful noise, was the tremendous accuracy'. He was sure the Germans were directing their fire from the top of the château, but he could do nothing about it.

Between explosions, Wally Parr dashed across the road to see Howard. 'I got a feeling', he panted, 'that there is somebody up there on that water tower, spotting for the Minnies'. He explained that the water tower, located near the maternity hospital, had a ladder up to the top, and that he could see something up there. Wouldn't Howard please give him permission to have a go at it? Howard agreed. 'And you couldn't see Wally's arse for dust', as Parr dashed back across the road to his gun.

Parr bellowed out, 'NUMBER ONE GUN!' As he did so, there was one of those strange lulls that occur in so many battles. In the silence Parr's booming voice carried across the battlefield, from Le Port to Benouville, from the canal to the river. Now, as Howard points out, there only was one gun; as Parr rejoins, it was the only substantial gun they had around the bridges at the time, so it really was the number one gun. Parr then put his crew through a drill that constituted a proper artilleryman's fire order. '700, One Round. Right 5 degrees', and so on, all orders proceeded by 'NUMBER ONE GUN'. Finally, 'PREPARE TO FIRE.' All around him, the soldiers – German as well as British – were fascinated spectators. 'FIRE!'

The gun roared, the shell hurtled off. It hit the water tower head-on. Great cheers went up, all around, berets and helmets were tossed into the air, men shook hands joyfully. The only trouble was, the shell was armour-piercing. It went in one side and came out the other without exploding. Streams of water began running out the holes, but the structure was still solid. Parr blasted away again, and again, until he had the tower spurting out water in every direction. Howard finally ordered him to quit.

112

When Gale, Kindersley, and Poett returned from their conference with Pine Coffin, they told Howard that one of his platoons would have to move up into Benouville and take a position in the line beside Taylor's company. Howard chose no. 1 platoon. He also sent Sweeney and Fox with their platoons over to the west side, to take a position across from the Gondrée café, where they should hold themselves ready to counter-attack in the event of a German breakthrough. 'And we thought', Sweeney says, 'that this was a little bit unfair. We'd had our battle throughout the night, Para had come in and taken over the position and we rather felt that we should be left alone for a little bit and that the 7th should not be calling on our platoons to come help it out.'

Sweeney and Fox settled down by a hedge. Back at Tarrant Rushton, a week earlier, Sweeney and Richard Todd had met, because of a confusion in their names – in the British army all Sweeneys were nicknamed Tod, and all Todds were known as Sweeney, after the famous barber in London, Sweeney Todd. On the occasion of their meeting, Sweeney and Todd laughed about the coincidence. Todd's parting words had been, 'See you on D-Day'. On the outskirts of Le Port, at 1100 hours on D-Day, as Sweeney rested against the hedge, 'a face appeared through the bushes and Richard Todd said to me, "I said I'd see you on D-Day", and disappeared again'.

Over in Benouville, no. 1 platoon was hotly engaged in street fighting. The platoon had gone through endless hours of practice in street fighting, in London, Southampton, and elsewhere, and had gained experience during the night, in the fighting around the café. Now it gave Taylor's company a much-needed boost, as it started driving Germans out of buildings they had recaptured.

Corporal Joe Caine was in command. 'He was a phlegmatic sort of a character', Bailey remembers; 'nothing seemed to perturb him'. They saw an outhouse in a small field. 'Cover me', Caine said to Bailey. 'I'm going to have a crap.'

He dashed off to the outhouse. A minute later he dashed back. 'I can't face that', Caine confessed. There was no hole in the ground, only a bucket, and nothing to sit on. The bucket looked as if it had not been emptied in weeks. It was overflowing. 'I can't face that', Caine repeated.

By about mid-day, most of the 7th Battalion had reported in for duty, some coming singly, some in small groups. Enough arrived so that Pine Coffin could release Howard's platoons. Howard brought them back to the area between the bridges. The snipers remained active, sporadically the Moaning Minnies showered down, battles were raging in Benouville, Le Port, and to the east of Ranville. D Company was shooting back at the snipers, but as Billy Gray confesses, 'We couldn't see them, we were just guessing'.

But limited though D Company's control was, it held the bridges.

CHAPTER EIGHT

D-Day: 1200 to 2400 hours

At noon, Sergeant Thornton was sitting in a trench, not feeling so good. He was terribly tired, of course, but what really bothered him was the situation. 'We were stuck there from twenty past twelve the night before, and the longer we were there, the more stuff there was coming over from Jerry, and we were in a small sort of circle and things were getting bloody hot, and the longer you sit anywhere, the more you start thinking. Some of them blokes were saying oh, I don't suppose I'll ever see the skies over England again, or the skies over Scotland or the skies over Wales or the skies over Ireland.' Wally Parr recalls, 'the day went on very, very, very wearing. All the time you could feel movement out there and closer contact coming.'

In Benouville and Le Port, 7th Battalion was holding its ground, but just barely. Major Taylor had survived the fire-fights of the night. He had also survived, shortly after dawn, the sight of a half-dozen prostitutes, shouting and waving and blowing kisses at his troops from the window of the room Private Bonck had vacated six hours earlier. By mid-day, the action had hotted up considerably, and Taylor not only had infantry and SPVs to deal with, but tanks.

'As the first tank crept round the corner', Taylor remembers, 'I said to my Piat man, "Wait, wait." Then, when it was about forty yards away, "Fire!" And he pulled the trigger, there was just a click, and he turned round and looked at me and said, "It's bent, sir".'

A corporal, seeing the situation, leapt out of his slit trench

115

and charged the tank, firing from the hip with his Sten. When he got to the tank, he slapped a Gammon bomb on it and ran off. The tank blew up and slithered across the road, blocking it.

Taylor, by this point, had a slashing splinter wound in his thigh. He managed to get up to a first-floor window, from which spot he continued to direct the battle. Richard Todd was half a mile away, but he heard Taylor shouting encouragement to his troops even at that distance. Nobody had any communications, the radios and field telephones having been lost on the drop. Taylor sent a runner over to Pine Coffin, to report that he had only thirty men left, most of them wounded, and could anything be done to help? That was when Pine Coffin told Howard to send a D Company platoon into Benouville.

There had as yet been no determined German armoured attacks – von Luck was still waiting for orders in his assembly area – which was fortunate for the paratroopers, as they had only Piats and Gammon bombs with which to fight tanks. But panzers could be expected at any time, coming down from Caen into Benouville, or perhaps up from the coast into Le Port.

The panzers had their own problems. Shortly after noon, von Luck was unleashed. Exactly as he had feared, his columns were immediately spotted and shelled. Over the course of the next couple of hours, his regiment was badly battered. On the west side of the Orne waterways, the other regiment of 21st Panzer Division also rolled into action, one part of it almost reaching Sword Beach, while one battalion moved off to attack Benouville.

None of these tanks was operating at anything like full efficiency because of the Allied air power and naval shelling. Lieutenant Werner Kortenhaus, who was in one of the tanks, reports that because of strafing activity by the RAF, the tanks had to advance with their hatches down. 'With only a narrow gap to look out through', he says, 'the panzer driver was almost always disorientated. We tended to go around in circles'. Thus the attacks lacked the coordinated punch they should have had.

In Le Port, Todd was trying to dislodge a sniper from the church tower. There was open ground around the church, 'so there was no way of rushing it, and anyway we had very few chaps on the ground at this time. So Corporal Killean, a young Irishman, volunteered to have a go and see if he could get there with his Piat. And he mouseholed through some cottages, going inside them and knocking holes through from one to the other so he was able to get to the end cottage. He ran out and got his Piat under a hedge and he let fly a bomb, and he hit a hole right where he wanted to in the church tower. He let off two more. And after a while he reckoned that he had indeed killed the sniper.'

Killean dashed to the church. But before entering, he took off his helmet and he said, 'I'm sorry to see what I have done to a wee house of God'.

Major Taylor kept glancing at his watch. Relief was supposed to arrive from the beaches, in the form of 3 Division or the Commandos, by noon. It was 1300 already, and neither 3 Division nor the Commandos had arrived. 'That was a very long wait', Taylor recalls. 'I know the longest day and all that stuff, but this really was a hell of a long day.' At his CP, which he had moved into the machine-gun pillbox after getting Bailey to clean up the mess he had made, Howard too kept checking the time, and wondering where the Commandos were.

In Oxford, Joy Howard was up shortly after dawn. She was so busy feeding and bathing and pottying the little ones that she did not turn on the radio. About 10 a.m. her neighbours, the Johnson's, knocked and told her that the invasion had started. 'We know Major Howard will be in it somewhere', they said, and insisted that Joy and the children join them for a celebration lunch. They lifted the baby chairs over the fence, and treated Joy to a brace of pheasants, a gift from friends in the country, and a bottle of vintage wine they had been saving for just this occasion.

Joy kept thinking of John's last words, that when she heard the invasion had started she would know that his job was done. They hardly gave her any comfort now, because she realised that for all she knew she was already a widow. As best she could, she put such thoughts out of her mind, and enjoyed the lunch. She spent the afternoon at her chores, but with her attention concentrated on the radio. She never heard John's name mentioned, but she did hear of the parachute drops on the eastern flank, and assumed John must be part of that.

Von Luck's panzers were rolling now, or rather moving forward as best they could through the exploding naval shells and the RAF strafing. Major Becker, the genius with vehicles who had built the outstanding SPV capability in von Luck's 125th Regiment, led the battle group descending on Benouville. His Moaning Minnies were firing as fast as he could reload them.

By 1300 the men at the bridge, and those in Benouville and Le Port, were beginning to feel disconcertingly like the settlers in the circled-up wagon train, Indians whooping all around them as they prayed for the cavalry to show up. They had enough ammunition to throw back probing attacks, but could not withstand an all-out assault – not alone anyway.

Tod Sweeney was gloomily considering the situation, sitting next to Fox. Suddenly he nudged Fox. 'Listen', he said. 'I can hear bagpipes.' Fox scoffed at this: 'Oh, don't be stupid, Tod, we're in the middle of France, you can't hear bagpipes.'

Sergeant Thornton, in his trench, told his men to listen, that he heard bagpipes. 'Go on', they replied, 'what are you talking about, you must be bloody nuts.' Thornton insisted that they listen.

Howard, at his CP, was listening intently. Back at Tarrant Rushton, he, Pine Coffin, and the commander of the Commandos, the legendary Lord Lovat, had arranged for recognition signals when they met in Normandy. Lovat, arriving by sea, would blow his bagpipes when he approached the bridge, to indicate that he was coming. Pine Coffin's bugler would blow back, with one call meaning the road in was clear, another that it was contested, and so on.

The sound of the bagpipe became unmistakable; Pine Coffin's bugler answered with a call that meant there was a fight going on around the bridges.

Lovat's piper, Bill Millin, came into view, then Lovat. It was a sight never to be forgotten. Millin was beside Lovat, carrying his great huge bagpipe and wearing his beret. Lovat had on his green beret, and a white sweater, and carried a walking stick, 'and he strode along', Howard remembers, 'as if he was on a flaming exercise back in Scotland'.

The Commandos came on, a Churchill tank with them. Contact had been made with the beachhead, and the men of D Company were ecstatic. 'Everybody threw their rifles down', Sergeant Thornton remembers, 'and kissing and hugging each other, and I've seen men with tears rolling down their cheeks. I did honestly. Probably I was the same. Oh, dear, celebrations I shall never forget.'

When Georges Gondrée saw Lovat coming, he got a tray, a couple of glasses, and a bottle of champagne then went dashing out of his café, shouting and crying. He caught up to Lovat, who was nearly across the bridge, and with a grand gesture offered him champagne. Lovat gave a simple gesture of 'No, thanks', in return, and marched on.

The sight was too much for Wally Parr. He ran out to Gondrée, nodding his head vigorously and saying, 'oui, oui, oui'. Gondrée, delighted, poured. 'Oh dear', Parr says, 'that was good champagne. Did it go down easy'.

Lovat met Howard at the east end of the bridge, piper Millin just behind him. 'John', Lovat said as they shook hands, 'today history is being made'. Howard briefed Lovat, telling him that once he got his troops over the canal bridge it was clear sailing. But, Howard warned, be careful going over the bridge. Lovat nevertheless marched his men across, and as a consequence had nearly a dozen casualties. Vaughan, who treated them, noted that most were shot through their berets and killed instantly. Commandos coming later put on their steel helmets to cross the bridge.

The last of the Commandos to pass through handed over to Howard a couple of bewildered-looking German soldiers, wearing only their underwear. They had run for it when D Company stormed the bridge, then hidden in a hedge along the canal towpath. When they saw the Commandos coming from the coast they decided it was time to give themselves up. A Commando Sergeant handed them over to Howard with a wide grin and said, 'Here you are, sir, a couple of the Panzoff Division!'

119

A few of the tanks coming up from the beaches went on into Benouville, where they set up a solid defensive line. Some crossed the bridges to go to Ranville and the east, to bolster the 6th Airborne Division in its fight against 21st Panzer Division.

The Germans tried a counter-attack coming straight up the canal. At about 1500 hours, a gun-boat came from Caen, loaded with troops. Bailey saw it first and alerted Parr, Gray and Gardner, manning the anti-tank gun. They had a heated discussion about range, but when they fired they were thirty yards short. The boat started to turn, they fired again, and hit the stern. The boat chugged off, back towards Caen, trailing smoke.

From about mid-afternoon onwards, the situation around the bridge stabilised. The 8th Heavy Grenadiers, and Major Becker's battle-group, had fought bitterly. But, as Kortenhaus admits, 'we failed because of heavy resistance. We lost thirteen tanks out of seventeen!' The Germans continued sniping and firing the Moaning Minnies, but they were no longer attacking in any strength.

'It was a beautiful evening', Nigel Taylor remembers. At about 1800 hours, when he was sure his position in Benouville was secure, he had himself carried down to the Gondrée café, so that he could be tended to at the aid post. When his leg wounds were bandaged he hobbled outside and sat at a table just beyond the front door. 'And Georges Gondrée brought me a glass of champagne, which was very welcome indeed after that sort of day, I can tell you. And then that evening, just before it got dark, there was a tremendous flight of aircraft, hundreds of British aircraft. They came in and they did a glider drop and a supply drop between the bridges and the coast on our side of the canal. It was a marvellous sight, it really was. They were also dropping supplies on chutes out of their bomb doors, and then it seemed only a very few minutes afterwards that all these chaps in jeeps, towing anti-tank guns and God knows what, were coming down the road through Le Port, and over this bridge.'

120

Taylor sipped his champagne, and felt good. 'At that moment I can remember thinking to myself, "My God, we've done it!" '

Among the gliders were the men of Brigadier Kindersley's Airlanding Brigade, D Company's parent outfit. The companies, with their heavy equipment, began moving across the bridge, towards Ranville and beyond to Escoville, which they were scheduled to attack that night or the following morning. As the Ox and Bucks marched past, Parr, Gray and the others called out, 'Where the hell you been?' and 'War's over', and 'A bit late for parade, chaps', and other such nonsense.

Howard's orders were to hand over to a seaborne battalion when it came up, then join the Ox and Bucks in Ranville. About midnight, the Warwickshire Regiment of 3 Division arrived. Howard briefed the commander. Parr handed over his anti-tank gun to a sergeant, showing him how to work it. 'I was a real expert on German artillery by this time', Parr says.

Howard told his men to load up. Someone found a horse cart – but no horse. The cart was a big, cumbersome thing, but the men had a lot to carry. All their own equipment, plus the German gear they had picked up (every soldier who could had changed his Enfield for a Schmeisser, or his Bren for an MG 34), filled the cart.

D Company started off, headed east, towards the river bridge and over it to Ranville. Howard was no longer under the command of Pine Coffin and Poett; he reverted to his regular chain of command and hereafter reported to his battalion colonel, Mike Roberts. He had carried out his orders, and almost exactly twenty-four hours after his men stormed the bridge, he handed over his objectives intact and secure.

Jack Bailey found it hard to leave. 'You see', he explains, 'we had been there a full day and night. We rather felt that this was our bit of territory'.

CHAPTER NINE

D-Day plus one to
D-Day plus ninety

Benouville was as far inland as the British seaborne units got on D-Day. The original plan had been to drive the armour coming in over the beaches right through Benouville, along the canal road, straight into Caen. But the fierceness of the opposition at Benouville and Le Port and Ranville convinced the British high command that prudence required going over to the defensive. And that was what they did for the next seven weeks, attempting only once – late in July, in Operation Goodwood – to break out.

D Company's role in this defensive phase of the battle was unspectacular. It had none of the excitement, or satisfaction that was inherent in the *coup de main* operation, but produced far higher casualties. D Company, in short, became an ordinary infantry company.

The process began just after midnight, in the first minutes of June 7. The company marched away from the bridges, pulling the cart loaded with the implements of war behind it. But the cart continually ran off the road, and the swearing, Jack Bailey says, was the most spectacular he ever heard. (And he became a regimental sergeant major in the post-war army, so he heard a lot.) Eventually, D Company gave up on the cart. Every man shouldered what he could, some of the equipment was left behind in the hated cart, and off they marched.

It was a depleted company that marched along towards Ranville. Howard had landed in Normandy twenty-four hours earlier with 181 officers and men. His battle casualties, considering that he had been in continuous action, were remarkably small – two men killed and fourteen wounded. One platoon remained unaccounted for.

His administrative losses, however, had been heavy. After unloading their gliders, and after the Commandos had opened a road, the glider pilots were under orders to go down to the beaches and use their special orders from Montgomery to get themselves back to England. In the afternoon, the pilots had done as ordered, depriving Howard of another ten men.* As communications improved between Benouville and the coast, his sappers were taken from him, to rejoin their parent units. That cost almost two dozen men. And as soon as the march ended, he would have to turn over Fox's and Smith's platoons to B Company – another forty men gone. His reinforced company in the early hours of June 6 had numbered 181; in the early hours of June 7 it numbered 76. And when Fox and Smith returned to B Company, Howard's only officer fit for duty was Sweeney. All the others were either dead, wounded, or missing.

D Company marched around Ranville. It was dark, there were numerous bends in the roads and a profusion of crossroads, and paratroopers scurrying in every direction. D Company got lost. Howard called for a break, then talked to Sweeney. He was worried that they had not met the regiment yet, and he did want to take the company down the road. 'Will you go ahead with a couple of chaps and see if you can make contact with the regiment, then come back here and report?'

Sweeney set off with Corporal Porter and one private. 'Herouvillette,' Sweeney reports, 'was a very eerie place. There were pigeons going in and out, and parachutists still dangling from buildings, dead bodies.' Sweeney was supposed to turn in Herouvillette, but he missed the turn, wandered about for an hour, finally found the right road, and set off for Ranville and the regiment.

One hundred yards down the road, he saw a dark shape ahead. Motioning for a quiet, careful advance, he moved towards it. There was a clang of a steel door, indicating a

---

*At the beach, Oliver Boland was interviewed by a newspaper reporter and gave a brief account of what happened at the canal bridge. *The Times* ran the article the next day, giving D Company its first publicity. There would be a great deal to follow.

German armoured vehicle ahead. Sweeney and his men had practised for exactly this situation during the years at Bulford. Sweeney pulled a grenade, threw it, and started running back towards Herouvillette, while Corporal Porter provided covering fire with his Bren gun.

Sweeney says, 'now the other chap was a big, slow farm lad who couldn't really run at all. He had never done anything athletic and as we were going down the road, he passed me, which I felt very upset about, this chap passing me. I said, "Here, private, wait for me". It seemed to me to be quite wrong that he should be racing past me down the road.'

The Germans, meanwhile, had sprung to life. Tracer bullets were whizzing past Sweeney and the private. Porter kept blazing away with his Bren. Sweeney and the private ducked behind a building to wait for Porter, but the fire-fight continued and Sweeney decided he had to report back to Howard, with or without Porter. Howard confessed to Sweeney that as he had listened to the fire-fight, his thought had been 'My God, there goes the last of my subalterns'.

Sweeney told Howard that there was no point in heading down the road. 'Wherever the regiment had got to it hasn't gone down the road towards Herouvillette and I've just run into an armoured car and lost Corporal Porter.' Howard agreed, saying that they would go back the other way and find the regiment. They did, and discovered that they had never been lost: the regiment had camped for the night in a different location from the one Howard had been told about. He had marched near it twice in the last two hours. It was 0300 hours.

When Howard reported to battalion headquarters, to his great delight he saw Brian Priday and Tony Hooper. They told him of how they had realised they were at the wrong bridge, how Hooper had become a prisoner and was then freed as Priday killed his captors with his Sten gun. They had set off cross-country, through swamps and over bogs, hiding in barns, engaging in fire-fights with German patrols, joining up with paratroopers, finally making it to Ranville. D Company now had twenty-two more men, and two more officers, including his second-in-command. Howard reorganised the company into three platoons, under the three remaining officers.

By 0400, the platoon commanders had put their men into German bunks, then found beds in a château for themselves. After two hours of sleep they were on the road by 0630. When it came to the road junction and the left turn towards Escoville, there was Corporal Porter sitting on the side of the road with his Bren gun. He looked at Sweeney and said, 'Where did you get to, sir?' Sweeney apologised but explained that he really had to get back and report.

D Company moved on towards Escoville when they suddenly came under very heavy fire. They took some casualties before setting out cross-country, and finally got to the farm Howard had picked as his company headquarters. He put his three platoons into position and they immediately came under mortar, SPV, tank, sniper and artillery fire. They were being attacked by the 2nd Panzer Grenadiers of von Luck's 125th Regiment of the 21st Panzer Division. 'And these people', Sweeney is frank to say, 'were a different kettle of fish to the people we had been fighting at the bridges'. Casualties were heavy, but D Company held its position.

About 1100 hours, Howard started to make another round of his platoons. Sweeney's was the first stop. Howard began studying the enemy with his German binoculars, 'then there was a zip and I was knocked out'. He had a hole right through his helmet, and there was enough blood to convince the men that he was mortally wounded.*

When that word went around in Sweeney's platoon, the men's reaction was to start organising patrols to find and kill the sniper who had shot their Major. In relating this incident, Tappenden commented: 'Every man in the company admired Major Howard more than almost anyone alive. He was a man who knew that if he couldn't do it, you couldn't do it, and you weren't asked to do it. We worshipped him and we wanted revenge'. Fortunately, Howard regained consciousness within a half hour – he had only been creased – and told the men to hold their positions.

By mid-afternoon, the Germans had pushed forward their attack, to the point that there were German tanks between

---

* Howard's helmet, complete with bullet-holes front and back, is now in the museum at Pegasus Bridge. He still bears the scar.

Hooper's platoon and the other two. Orders came down from battalion to withdraw to Herouvillette. The retreat was carried out in fairly good order, considering the pressure and considering that Howard had lost nearly half his fighting strength in half a day.

Parr and Bailey covered the retreat. When they pulled back behind a château, Parr gasped out to the Padre standing there with the wounded, 'Let's get going. They are right behind us.' The Padre replied that he was going to stay with the wounded, be taken prisoner with them, so that he could be with them in their POW camp. Bailey and Parr organised some of the men, found some improvised stretchers, and carried the wounded back to Herouvillette. 'It wasn't far', Parr says, 'only three-quarters of a mile'.

When they got there, the rest of the men were lined up in the ditch all facing the direction from which the Germans would be attacking. 'And the sergeant major, almost with tears in his eyes, was striding up and down and saying in a great booming voice, "Well done, lads. Well done. Wait till the bastards come at us this time. We'll mow 'em down. I'm proud of you. Well done." ' It was a scene more reminiscent of World War I than World War II.

When the Germans did come, D Company mowed them down as if it was the Battle of Mons all over again. But that only highlighted the transformation that had taken place in D Company's role. On June 6 it had been at the cutting edge of tactical innovation and technological possibilities. On June 7 it was fighting with the same tactics ordinary infantry companies used throughout the First World War.

Howard set up headquarters in Herouvillette, and the company stayed there for four days. They were always under attack by mortar and artillery fire, sometimes having to fight off tanks and infantry. By the end of four days, they were down to less than fifty fighting men.

The company moved twice more, then settled down into defensive positions it was to hold for almost two months. 'The only thing we could do was to send out fighting patrols every night to bring back prisoners', Howard says. On one patrol he took with Wally Parr, they found themselves in the area where the Battle of Breville had just been fought. In the moonlight they could see the scattered corpses of men who had been killed by an artillery concentration. Howard and Parr found one group of six men, sitting in a circle in their half-completed slit-trench, playing cards. They were still sitting up, holding their cards, and they had no bullet or shrapnel wounds. But they were all dead, killed by concussion.

During this period, Howard says, 'the biggest problem I had was keeping up the morale of the troops because we had always got the impression that we would soon be withdrawn from Normandy to come back and refit in the UK for another airborne operation'. After all, the glider pilots had been withdrawn and were already in England.

Another morale problem came from the constant shelling. 'Chaps began to go bomb-happy', Howard says.

At first many of us tended to regard it as a form of cowardice and we were highly critical. I remember that I tended to take a very tough and almost unfeeling line about it. But after a time, when we began to see some of our best and most courageous comrades going under, we soon changed our minds. We could see that it was a real sickness. Men would hide away and go berserk during bombardments, and they became petrified during attacks. They could not be used for patrols, or even sentry duty, and the only answer was to hand them over to the Medical Officer, who, once he was satisfied it was a genuine case, had the man evacuated as a casualty. It was pathetic to see good men go down.

Howard himself almost went under. By D-Day plus four, he had gone for five days with almost no sleep, and his losses in Escoville and Herouvillette were heartrending. 'I felt terribly depressed and pessimistic', Howard admits, 'feeling quite sure that the Allied bridgehead was going to collapse on our vulnerable left flank. However, once the CO and the MO persuaded me what was wrong, with quiet threats of evacuation, I luckily shook myself out of it. It was an awful experience.'

Howard learned a lesson from the experience. He got

regular, if short, periods of sleep for himself, and he saw to it that the platoon leaders arranged regular rest periods for everyone in turn, especially after attack or shell fire. Another manifestation of the pressure was some self-inflicted wounds, shots through the leg or foot 'usually said to have occurred when cleaning weapons. They were very difficult to prove.' Howard found that keeping up morale when casualties are heavy is always difficult and he did what he could. 'Good discipline and *esprit de corps* goes a long way towards over-coming it, but I found keeping the men well occupied was as good a cure as any. Active aggressive patrolling, sniping parties, marches behind the line and above all keep everyone in the picture. Glean all you can from HQ by way of information about how the battle is going and have regular meetings with the men to pass it on.'

Howard went to HQ not only to find out what was going on, but to do all those little things a good company commander does. He made certain there were plenty of cigarettes, for example, with an extra supply after a battle or a shelling. He also ensured the prompt arrival and distribution of the mail ('Essential for maintaining good morale'), sending runners back to HQ for the mail if he thought he could save a few minutes. Getting fresh bread was another morale-booster, though the first shipment did not arrive until about D plus 25. 'I was astounded over how much we longed for it.'

Cleaning weapons became almost an obsession. First thing in the morning, after the dawn stand to and breakfast, everything came out – rifles, machine-guns, Piats, mortars, grenades, ammunition – and everything was cleaned, oiled and inspected. Many of the men had a Schmeisser by this time.

During this period, Howard says, 'one thing I could never get used to were the smells of battle. Worst of these was dead and putrefying bodies. The men, friend and foe, were buried, but there was dead livestock everywhere just rotting away. In the middle of summer it was hell. At one château a stable full of wonderful racehorses was caught in a burning building. The appalling smell from that place spread over a very wide area, and it was sickening. We eventually dealt with it by loads of lime, but you can imagine the flies that pyre attracted.'

But the biggest morale problem of all was a nagging question in every man's mind: 'Why are we being wasted like this? Surely there must be other bridges between here and Berlin that will have to be captured intact.'

It is indeed a mystery why the War Office squandered D Company, a unique group in the British army. Huge sums had been spent on its training, and its combination of training, skills, and hand-picked officers was unsurpassed.

Despite all this, the War Office sacrificed D Company to the German guns. Sweeney was wounded, Priday was wounded, Hooper was wounded – by August none of D Company's original officers were left, save Howard himself. All the sergeants and the sergeant-major were gone. Thornton had a leg wound and had been evacuated; so had Parr.

On D plus 11, Howard was wounded again, receiving shrapnel in his back. His driver took him back to an aid post where a surgeon removed it, and when he finished, the doctor told Howard to lie there for a while. Mortar rounds started coming in, and everybody ran for cover. Howard looked around. He was alone in the farmhouse operating-room. He jumped off the table, put on his shirt and battle smock, and went outside. Finding his driver taking shelter under the jeep, he told him, 'Let's get back to the company. It's quieter there than it is here.'

Howard's return to the front lines was followed by some confusion as to his whereabouts. All the documentation at the aid post showed that he had been evacuated to England, and as a result his mail was diverted to hospital there. The daily letters he had been getting from Joy suddenly stopped coming. This was the period when V1s and V2s were raining down on England and he was tortured with thoughts of her death and the loss of his children. That experience, Howard says, 'nearly sent me round the bend'.

It was worse for Joy. She got a telegram from the War Office which was supposed to read, 'Your husband has suffered a mortar wound and is in hospital'. In fact it read, 'Your husband has suffered a mortal wound and is in hospital'. A frantic Joy was told that he was in such-and-such hospital. She called there and was told he never arrived. No one knew where he was. For two weeks before the matter was worked out, and they started receiving letters from each other again, John and Joy suffered terribly.

Sergeant Hickman was fighting across from D Company once again. He gives a description of what it was like from the German point of view:

> There was man-to-man fighting, fighting in the rubble along the streets. You didn't know who was running in front of you and who was running behind you, you couldn't recognise anything and everybody ran. In the daytime we took position, and night we moved either to the left, to the right, back. I had a map case in my belt. The map made no difference to me because I didn't know where I was. So you were moved two kilometres to the left, two kilometres to the right, three kilometres forwards, or back again. Every day you counted your men, one section had two men left, another three. I was a platoon commander with five men to command.

On September 2, while trying to swim the Orne River, Hickman was wounded, captured, interrogated, and sent on to a POW camp in England.

Von Luck was also having a bad time. Every two or three days he would launch armoured attacks, but every time his tanks moved, observers in balloons would spot him, radio to the big ships offshore and the planes overhead, and down would come naval gunfire and strafing Spitfires.

On July 18, there was the biggest bombardment von Luck ever experienced, from bombers, naval warships, and artillery. This was part of operation Goodwood, designed to break through the German lines, capture Caen, and drive on towards Paris. As the barrage moved past him, von Luck set out for the front on his motorcycle. He arrived at a battery of smoking 88mm guns pointing skyward, commanded by a Luftwaffe major. Off to his right, less than a kilometre away, von Luck could see twenty-five British tanks moving forward. He pointed them out to the battery commander and said, 'Major, depress your guns and kill those tanks'. The major refused. He said he was a Luftwaffe officer, and his target was bombers, not tanks. Von Luck repeated his order. Same response.

Von Luck pulled his pistol, pointed it between the major's eyes at a six-inch range, and said, 'Major, in one minute you are either a dead man or you will have won a medal'. The major depressed his guns, started shooting, and within minutes had crippled twenty-five British tanks. Shortly thereafter, Monty called off operation Goodwood.

In late August, 21st Panzer Division was pulled out of the Normandy battle. Von Luck and his men were sent over to the Rhône Valley to meet the threat of the invading forces in southern France.

At the end of August the British broke through and had the Germans on the run. D Company was part of the pursuit. It reached a village near the Seine, where Howard established his headquarters in a school and received the schoolmaster. The Frenchman said he wanted to show some appreciation for being liberated. 'But I've got nothing of any value that I can give you', he confessed to Howard. 'The Germans took everything of value before they left, in prams and God knows what, but the one thing I can give you is my daughter.'

And bringing out his eighteen-year-old daughter, he offered her to Howard. 'It was so pathetic', Howard remembers. He declined, but he also thinks the schoolmaster passed his daughter on down to the other ranks – and that they accepted the gift.

The following day, on the Seine itself, Howard came into a village 'where we saw all these girls with all their hair cut off and tied to a lamp post. It was a gruesome sight, really.' He wondered if that kind of humiliation was being handed out to the prostitutes back in Benouville, who had been as eager to please the British troops as they had the Germans. Or to the young mothers in the maternity hospital. Whose babies could those be, anyway, with all able-bodied Frenchmen off in slave labour or POW camps?

Howard thought it unfair of the French to take out all their

131

frustrations on a single segment of society. Almost everyone in France had got through the German occupation by doing whatever it was that he or she did quietly and without a fuss. One of the things young girls do is establish romantic attachments with young boys, and there were only young German boys around. The girls had no choice, but to Howard's dismay they had to bear the brunt of the first release of pent-up outrage following the liberation celebration. Those Frenchmen with guilty consciences did most of the hair cutting.

On September 5, after three months of continuous combat, D Company was withdrawn from the lines. It travelled by truck to Arromanches, was driven out to Mulberry Harbour, climbed up scramble nets aboard ships, and set sail for Portsmouth. Then by truck to Bulford, where the members of the company moved back into their old rooms and took stock of their losses. Howard was the only officer still with them. All the sergeants and most of the corporals were gone. D Company had fallen from its D-Day strength of 181 to 40.

CHAPTER TEN

D-Day plus three months to D-Day plus forty years

After one night at Bulford, the company went on leave. Howard drove up to Oxford for a reunion with his family and a glorious rest. On the morning of September 17, he relates, 'I got up and saw all these planes milling around with gliders on them, and of course I knew that something was on'. The planes were headed for Arnhem. Howard knew that Jim Wallwork and the other pilots were up there, and he silently wished him good luck.

Howard did not know it, but Sergeant Thornton was also up there, with a stick of paratroopers. When Thornton was evacuated from Normandy, he had a quick recovery from his wound. Then, rather than wait for the Ox and Bucks to return, he had transferred to the 1st Airborne Division, gone through his jump training, and was going in with Colonel John Frost's 2nd Battalion. Thornton fought beside Frost at Arnhem bridge for four days, and was captured with him.

Howard could hardly imagine such a thing, but none of those gliders overhead carried *coup de main* parties, not for the bridge at Arnhem, nor the one at Nijmegen. It seems possible that had D Company been available, someone would have thought to lay on *coup de main* parties for the bridges. If they had been there to take the bridge at Nijmegen, the American paratroopers would not have had to fight a desperate battle for it. Rather, they could have set up a defensive perimeter, with the strength to spare to

133

send men over to Arnhem to help out. At Arnhem, with glider help, Frost could have held both ends of his bridge, greatly simplifying his problems.

But it was not to be. D Company had not been pulled out of Normandy until it was an exhausted, battered, remnant of its old self, and evidently no other company could take its place. Certainly there were no *coup de main* parties in the gliders over Howard's head. He watched them straighten out and then head east, and he again wished them good luck.

In late September, 1944, ten days after Arnhem, Howard reported back to Bulford and set out to rebuild D Company, brought up to full strength by reinforcements. Howard's job was to make the recruits into genuine airborne soldiers. He started with basics – physical and weapon training. By mid-November, he was ready to take the recruits on street-fighting exercises, to get his men accustomed to live ammunition. He selected an area of Birmingham, arranged for bunks for the men, and returned to Bulford.

On Friday, November 13, Howard decided to spend the night with Joy, as Oxford was on the route to Birmingham. He brought with him two Oxford residents, Corporal Stock and his new second-in-command, Captain Osborne, together with his batman. Although Stock was his driver, Howard insisted on taking the wheel, because, although a good driver, Stock did not drive fast enough.

At about 5:30, just as dusk was falling, they met a Yank convoy of six-ton trucks on a narrow, twisting road. They were on a right hand bend. Suddenly, with no warning, Howard 'saw this six-ton truck in front of me. He'd lost his place in the convoy and he was obviously leap-frogging up, and it was all over so quickly.'

They had a head-on crash. Howard was jammed behind the steering-wheel, and both legs, his right hip, and his left knee were smashed up. Osborne suffered lesser injuries, but the other two escaped with cuts and bruises.

Howard was taken to hospital in Tidworth, where he was on the critical list for nearly six weeks. Joy made many long journeys to visit him. In December, using his connections with the Oxford police, Howard got himself moved to the Wingfield hospital in Oxford. He remained there until March, 1945.

D Company went on to fight in the Battle of the Bulge, then led the way on the Rhine crossing and participated in the drive to the Baltic. Most of the glider pilots were at Arnhem, then flew again in the Rhine crossing.

When Howard came out of hospital, he was using crutches. By the time his convalescent leave was nearly over, so was the war in Europe. But when he reported for duty, he learned that the Ox and Bucks were going to the Far East for another glider operation. The battalion commander asked Howard if he could get fit in time. It seemed the authorities wanted to promote him and make him second-in-command of the battalion.

Howard immediately started a training programme on a track near his home. On the second day of trying to run laps, his right hip seized up and the leg went dead. He had not allowed his injuries to heal properly, and the strain on the hip from the running caused it to jam, which stopped the nerves running down the leg. Howard went back into hospital for further operations. When he got out this time, the war in Asia was over.

He wanted to stay in the army, make a career of it, 'but before I knew where I was I was kicked out of the army, invalided out. My feet just didn't touch'.

Howard went into the Civil Service, first with the National Savings Committee, then with the Ministry of Food, and finally with the Ministry of Agriculture. In 1946 he had an audience with the King at Buckingham Palace. On June 6, 1954, the tenth anniversary of D-Day, he received a Croix de Guerre avec Palme from the French government, which had already renamed the bridge. From that day onward, its name has been 'Pegasus Bridge'. Later the road between the bridge and the LZ was named 'Esplanade John Howard'.

Howard served as a consultant for Darryl Zanuck in the making of the film, *The Longest Day*. Played by Richard Todd, he had a prominent role in the film, which of course delighted him. He was less happy about Zanuck's penchant for putting drama ahead of accuracy: Zanuck insisted that there *had* to be explosives in place under the bridge, and it was he, not

Howard, who prevailed at the bridge on this occasion. In the film, the sappers are seen pulling out explosives from under the bridge and throwing them into the canal. Zanuck also romanticised the arrival of Lovat and his Commandos, quite falsely depicting their bagpipes playing as they crossed Pegasus Bridge.

Howard retired in 1974, and he and Joy live in a small but comfortable home in the tiny village of Burcot, about eight miles from Oxford. Terry and Penny live close enough for the grandchildren to pay regular visits. The Howards do not travel much, but John manages to return to Pegasus Bridge almost every year on June 6. His hip and legs are so mangled that he needs a walking-stick to get around, and then only moves with great pain, but all his enormous energy flows out again when he sees his bridge, and greets Madame Gondrée, and starts talking to those of his men who have made it over for this particular anniversary. Sweeney and Bailey are usually there, and sometimes Wood and Parr and Gray and always some of the others.

Von Luck spent the remainder of the autumn of 1944 fighting General Le Clerc's French armoured division. In mid-December he was involved in the fighting at the southern end of the Battle of the Bulge, and was surprised at how much the Americans had improved since February, 1943, when he had fought them at Kasserine Pass. In the spring of 1945, 21st Panzer went to the Eastern front, to join in the defence of Berlin. In late April, by then encircled, von Luck was ordered to break through the Russian lines, then hold it open so that Ninth Army could get out and surrender to the Americans. Before attacking the Russians, von Luck called what was left of his regiment together, and gave a small talk.

'We are here now', he began, 'and I think that it is more or less the end of the world. Please forget about the Thousand Year Reich. Please forget all about that. You will ask, Why then are we going to fight again? I tell you, there's only one reason you are fighting, it is for your families, your grounds, your homeland. Always think about what will happen when the Russians overcome your wives, your little daughters, your village, your homeland.'

The men fought until they were out of ammunition, and von Luck told them, 'Now it's finished, you are free to go wherever you want'. Von Luck himself went to report to the commander of the Ninth Army, and was captured by the Russians. They sent him to a POW camp in the Caucasus, where he spent five years as a coal miner. In 1951 he moved to Hamburg, where he became a highly successful coffee importer.

Beginning in the mid-1970s, the Swedish royal military academy has brought von Luck and Howard together to give talks on Normandy battles and leadership. They hit it off from the first, and have grown to like each other more with each annual appearance. Today they could only be described as very good friends. 'So much for war', Howard comments.

Sergeant Hickman spent the remainder of the war in England as a POW. He liked the country so much that when he was shipped home, he applied for a visa. It was granted, and he emigrated to England, changing his name to Henry, and got a job, married a British woman, and settled down. One day in the early 1960s one of his friends at work told him that there was a British parachute reunion going on that night, and as an old paratrooper himself he might want to attend. Hickman did. There he saw Billy Gray, the same man he had faced at 0020 hours on June 6, 1944, in front of the café, with his machine-gun blazing away.

Hickman did not recognise Gray, but during the evening Gray pulled out some photographs of Pegasus Bridge and started to explain the *coup de main*. Hickman looked at the photos. 'I know that bridge', he said. He and Gray got talking. Later they exchanged visits, and a friendship developed. Over the years it grew closer and deeper, and today they are intimates. They kid each other about what lousy marksmen they were in their youth. 'So much for war.'

General Sir Nigel Poett, KCB, DSO, had a distinguished military career. Now retired, he lives near Salisbury. Major Nigel Taylor, MC, is a solicitor living near Malvern. Richard Todd continues to pursue his highly successful acting career. Major Dennis Fox, MBE, soldiered on for ten years after the war, then became an executive with ITV. Colonel H. J.

137

Sweeney, MC, also stayed in the army until he was fifty-five; today he is the Director-General of the Battersea Dogs' Home near Old Windsor, and the head of the Ox and Bucks regimental veterans' association.

Major R. A. A. Smith, MC, became a director of both Shell and BP in India; he is now retired but runs tours to India. Colonel David Wood, MBE, soldiered on until retirement. He organised staff college visits to Pegasus, where Howard and Taylor would give lectures on what happened. Today David lives in retirement in Devon.

Staff Sergeant Oliver Boland, Croix de Guerre, lives in retirement near Stratford-upon-Avon. Jack Bailey stayed in the army, where he became a regimental sergeant major. Today he is head clerk in a London firm and lives in Catford, near Wally Parr. Dr John Vaughan has a medical practice in Devon.

Staff Sergeant Jim Wallwork, DFM, worked as a salesman for the first ten years after the war. In 1956 he emigrated to British Columbia, where today he runs a small livestock farm on the edge of the mountains east of Vancouver. From his porch, and from his picture window, Jim has a grand view of a valley dropping away before him. The kind of view a glider pilot gets on his last approach to the LZ.

Corporal Wally Parr wanted to stay in the army, but with a wife and children decided he had to get out. He returned to Catford, where one of his sons is in his window-cleaning business with him. Another son is a promising musician.

To my knowledge, there are no intact Horsa gliders flying today. Zanuck got the blueprints and built one for *The Longest Day*, but was told by the Air Ministry that the design was inherently bad and the craft not air-worthy. Therefore Zanuck could not fly it across the Channel, as he had hoped to do, but had to dismantle the thing, bring it over by ship, and put it together again in France.

The model of the bridge and surrounding area, the one that Howard and his men studied so intently in Tarrant Rushton, is today in the Parachute Regiment Museum at Aldershot.

Benouville has a few new houses, some development, but

basically it is as it was on June 6, 1944. So is Ranville, where Den Brotheridge is buried, under a tree in the churchyard.

The Gondrée café remains, changed only by the portraits on the wall of John Howard, Jim Wallwork, Nigel Taylor, and the others who came to liberate France and the Gondrées.

Madame Gondrée presides over her tiny café in a grand fashion. To see her on a June 6, surrounded by her many friends from D Company and from the 7th Battalion, chatting away gaily, remembering the great day however many years ago, is to see a happy woman. Before he died in the late 1960s, her husband Georges made many close British friends, Howard especially. Jack Bailey went duck hunting with Gondrée each year.

When asked to describe life during the occupation, Madame Gondrée lets loose a torrent of words, paragraphs or incidents separated by heartfelt cries of 'Mon Dieu! Mon Dieu!' She still hates the Germans and will not allow them into her café today. When Zanuck was shooting *The Longest Day*, he wanted to have half-dressed German soldiers come leaping out of the windows of the café as D Company charged across the bridge. Madame screamed, insisting to Zanuck that she had never, never had Germans sleeping in her house, and that he absolutely must take that scene out of the script. Unlike Howard, Madame got her way. The scene was dropped.

When Howard goes to the café today, he sometimes brings Hans von Luck with him. Howard has told Madame that von Luck might look suspiciously like a German, but that he is in fact a Swede.

The canal has been widened by some four or five feet. The château stands intact. The machine-gun pillbox that Jack Bailey knocked out and John Howard used as a CP is still there, forming the foundation of the house lived in by the man who operates the swing-bridge. The bunkers are all filled in. But the anti-tank gun and its emplacement, where Wally Parr had so much fun, remains. Three stone markers are placed on the sites where the three gliders crashed.

The river bridge is a new one, built since the war. The canal bridge, Pegasus Bridge, is still there.

The significance of Pegasus Bridge

Pegasus Bridge today plays only a minor role in the Norman economy. It is lightly used, and for local purposes exclusively, because all the long-distance or heavy commercial traffic uses the new autoroute that runs from Le Havre to Caen to Bayeux. But on June 6, the bridge recalls its former glory, the day on which it was the most important bridge in Normandy. The tourists and the veterans come in increasing numbers each year to visit the museum and the Gondrée café, the bridge, the markers designating the landing sites of the gliders. They are keenly interested in the operation, and want to know how the British did it.

There was no single key to the success of Howard's *coup de main,* or to the success of the 5th Para Brigade in providing relief just when it was most needed. Success in this case truly had many parents. John Howard stands out, of course, but without Jim Wallwork, Howard might well have come to earth miles from the bridge, or even on the wrong river. And so it goes, down the line. Gale's contribution was absolutely critical, but then so was Poett's. Without the information George Gondrée fed the British, and without the air reconnaissance photographs, D Company might well have failed. If Nigel Taylor had not got his company into Benouville in time, or fought so magnificently once there, all would have been for nought. So too for Sergeant Thornton, without whose Piat all would have been in vain. If Jack Bailey had not knocked out the pillbox, Howard could hardly have taken, much less held, the bridge.

There were, in short, many heroes, each making a key contribution to the final success. If any one of these men – and in fact many others – had failed, the mission as a whole would have failed. Rather than single out individuals for praise, therefore, it is more appropriate to attempt an analysis of the factors in the British success.

TRAINING: It would be hard to find any company in the entire history of warfare that was better trained for a single operation than D company was on D-Day. Major Howard had laid the base in 1942 and 1943 by getting his men into the fittest physical condition possible, teaching them all the skills of combat infantry, forcing them to become accustomed to fighting at night, drilling into them patterns of quick response and immediate reactions. Then in the spring of 1944, he put them through the drill of capturing the bridges innumerable times. When they went into the operation, the men of D Company were far better trained for the battle that ensued than their opponents were. And their *esprit de corps* was as good as that to be found anywhere in the British army.

PLANNING AND INTELLIGENCE: The quality of British planning, like the intelligence on which it was based, was outstanding. Possibly no company commander in any invading force has ever known so much about his opposition as John Howard knew. On the basis of this intelligence, General Gale came up with a plan that was both highly professional and brilliant. Poett added his own touches to his part of the plan, as did Howard. It could not have been better conceived.

EXECUTION: The execution of the operation was somewhat less than perfect. Because of a navigation error, one-sixth of Howard's fighting strength never got into the battle. Howard's emphasis on having his platoon commanders lead from the front cost him dearly – in retrospect it certainly seems a mistake to have Lieutenants Brotheridge and Smith lead their platoons over the bridge, or to have Lieutenant Wood lead his platoon in clearing out the trenches. The paratroop drop was much too scattered, causing a delay in the arrival of reinforcements at critical moments. Coordination between ground and air for strafing and bombing support was sadly lacking. Radio communications were poor.

The things that went right were, obviously, of more significance. First and foremost, the achievement of the glider pilots was crucial, unprecedented, and magnificent. Second, the way in which D Company recovered from the shock of the landing and went about its drill exactly as planned was outstanding. Third, the night-fighting and street-fighting ability of D Company proved far superior to that of the enemy. Fourth, although the paras may have been understrength when they arrived, and a bit late at that, they did get there in time and did outfight the Germans, even though the Germans heavily outnumbered and outgunned them. Fifth, although Howard lost a majority of his officers and NCOs early on, he had the company so well trained that corporals and privates were able to undertake critical missions on their own intiative.

SURPRISE: Without surprise, obviously, there could have been no success. Any kind of a warning, even just two or three minutes before 0016, would have been sufficient for the Germans. Had Major Schmidt's garrison been alert when D Company landed, every man in the three gliders could have been killed by machine-gun fire before any got out. Surprise was complete, both with regard to method and target.

LUCK: Give me generals who are lucky said Napoleon, and so says every commander since. Howard and the British had more than their share of good luck. The best, probably, was the bomb that did not explode when it hit the bridge. (One is tempted to think that this was not just luck; it is at least possible that the bomb had been deliberately sabotaged by a French slave labourer in a German munitions factory.) It certainly was good luck that Thornton's Piat bomb set off the explosions inside the tank near the T junction. And it was wonderfully lucky that Hitler did not release the 21st Panzer Division to attack until after noon on D-Day.

METHOD: In his May 2 orders to Howard, Poett had said that the capture of the bridges would depend on 'surprise, speed, and dash for success'. In the event, Howard and D Company showed all three characteristics in carrying out their assignment.

What did it all mean? Because the operation was a success, we can never know its full significance; only if it had failed would we know the real value of Pegasus Bridge. As it is, any assessment of the operation's worth is speculative. But then speculation is the secret vice of every history buff, and in any case is unavoidable when passing judgements.

Suppose, then, that Major Schmidt had managed to blow the bridges. In that event, even if Howard's men held both sides of both waterways, the easy movement that the British enjoyed over the bridges would have been impossible. Howard could not have brought Fox's platoon over from the river to Benouville, and Thornton would not have been by the T junction with his Piat. The most likely outcome, in that case, would have been a failure to hold the ground in the Benouville-Le Port area, with the resulting isolation of the 6th Airborne east of the Orne. Had German tanks come down to the bridge from Benouville, the enemy surely would have repulsed the invaders. In that case, with the bridges in German hands, the 6th Airborne would have been isolated, in a position comparable to that of the 1st Airborne later in the war in Arnhem.

The loss of a single division, even a full-strength, elite division like the 6th Airborne, could by itself hardly have been decisive in a battle that raged over a sixty-mile front and involved hundreds of thousands of men. But 6th Airborne's mission, like the division itself, was special. Eisenhower and Montgomery counted on General Gale to hold back the Germans on the left, making him the man most responsible for preventing the ultimate catastrophe of panzer formations loose on the beaches, rolling them up one by one. Gale was able to hold off the German armour, thanks in critical part to the possession of Pegasus Bridge.

Denying the use of the bridges to the Germans was important in shaping the ensuing campaign. As Hitler began bringing armoured divisions from the Pas de Calais to Normandy, he found it impossible to launch a single, well-coordinated blow. There were two major reasons. First, Allied air harassment and the activities of the French Resistance slowed the movement to the battlefield. Second, the only area available to the Germans

143

to form up for such a blow was the area between the Dives and the Orne. The natural line of attack would have been over Pegasus Bridge, down to Ouistreham, then straight west along the beaches. But because the 6th Airborne controlled Pegasus Bridge, such divisions as the 2nd Panzer, the 1st SS Panzer, and the famous Panzer Lehr, had been forced to go around bombed-out Caen, then enter the battle to the west of that city. As a consequence, they went into battle piecemeal and against the front, not the flank, of the main British forces. In the seven-week battle that followed, the Germans attacked again and again, using up the cream and much of the bulk of their armoured units in the process.

At a minimum, then, failure at Pegasus Bridge would have made D-Day much more costly to the Allies, and especially to the 6th Airborne Division. At a maximum, failure at Pegasus Bridge might have meant failure for the invasion as a whole.

There was one other matter of significance about Pegasus Bridge that needs to be mentioned. Dwight Eisenhower used to say that no totalitarian dictatorship could ever match the fighting fury of an aroused democracy. That was certainly true in this case. The Germans provided their men with better weapons than the British had available; they also put more men into the battle. But with the exception of a handful of fanatic Nazis, none of those wearing German uniforms in and around Pegasus Bridge (no matter what country they came from) wanted to be there. In the case of D Company and the 5th Para Brigade, every man who was there was a volunteer who wanted desperately to be there. In addition, the Germans were badly hampered by the mistrust that prevailed among their high command. Jealousy and suspicion are common in all high commands in war, of course, but nowhere else did they go so far as in Nazi Germany. The direct consequence for Pegasus Bridge was the holding back of 21st Panzer until after Hitler had woken, a disastrous delay.

By contrast, the British high command trusted General Gale and allowed him wide leeway in meeting his objectives. Gale trusted Poett; Poett trusted Kindersley and Pine Coffin; they all trusted John Howard; Howard trusted his subalterns. In every instance, superiors left details of operations to the man on the spot.

The common soldiers of the Third Reich were almost incapable of acting on their own. Deprived of their officers and NCOs, they tended to fade away into the night. Whereas British soldiers – men like Jack Bailey and Wally Parr and Billy Gray and Wagger Thornton – were eager to seize the initiative, quick to exploit an opportunity, ready to act on their own if need be.

It is, therefore, possible to claim that the British won the Battle of Pegasus Bridge primarily because the army they sent into the fray was better than the enemy army, and it was better precisely because it represented a democratic rather than a totalitarian society. Ultimately, then, the victory was one for freedom, won by an army of the free.

Appendix: Poett's orders to Howard

5 Para Bde 00 No. 1 Appx. A

Ref Maps. 1/50,000 Sheets 7/F1, 7/F2   TOP SECRET
         1/25,000 Sheet No. 40/16 NW   *2 May 44*

To: Maj R. J. Howard, 2 Oxf Bucks
INFM
1 Enemy

(a) Static def in area of ops.

Garrison of the two brs at BENOUVILLE 098748 and RANVILLE 104746 consists of about 50 men, armed with four LAA guns, probably 20 mm, four to six LMG, one AA MG and possibly two A Tk guns of less than 50 cm cal. A concrete shelter is under constr, and the br will have been prepared for demolition. See ph enlargement A21.

(b) Mobile res in area of ops.

One bn of 736 GR is in the area LEBISEY 0471 – BIEVILLE 0674 with probably 8 to 12 tks under comd. This bn is either wholly or partially carried in MT and will have at least one coy standing by as an anti-airtpo picket.

Bn HQ of the RIGHT coastal bn of 736 GR is in the area 065772. At least one pl will be available in this area as a fighting patrol, ready to move out at once to seek infm.

(c) State of Alertness.

The large scale preparations necessary for the invasion of the Continent, the suitability of moon and tide will combine to produce a high state of alertness in the GERMAN def. The br grn may be standing to, and charges will have been laid in the demolition chambers.

(d) Detailed infm on enemy def and res is available on demand from Div Int Summaries, air phs and models.

146

2 **Own Tps**
   (a) 5 Para Bde drops immediately NE of RANVILLE at H minus 4 hrs 30 mins, and moves forthwith to take up a def posn round the two brs.
   (b) 3 Para Bde drops at H minus 4 hrs 30 mins and is denying to the enemy the high wooded ground SOUTH of LE MESNIL 1472.
   (c) 6 Airldg Bde is ldg NE of RANVILLE and WEST of BENOUVILLE at about H plus 12 hrs, and moves thence to a def posn in the area STE HONORINE LA CHARDON-NERETTE 0971 – ESCOVILLE 1271.
   (d) 3 Br Div is ldg WEST of OUISTREHAM 1079 at H hr with objective CAEN.

3 **Ground**
   See available maps, air ph and models.

INTENTION
4 Your task is to seize *intact* the brs over R ORNE and canal at BENOUVILLE 098748 and RANVILLE 104746, and to hold them until relief by 7 Para Bn. If the brs are blown, you will est personnel ferries over both water obstacles as soon as possible.

METHOD
5 **Composition of force**
   (a) Comd   Maj RJ HOWARD 2 OXF BUCKS
   (b) Tps   D Coy 2 OXF BUCKS less sp Brens and 3"M dets.
            two pls B Coy 2 OXF BUCKS
            det of 20 Sprs 249 Fd Coy (Airborne)
            det 1 Wing Glider P Regt

6 **Flight plan**
   (a) HORSA gliders available 6.
   (b) LZ X. triangular fd 099745. 3 gliders.
       LZ Y. rectangular fd 104747. 3 gliders.
   (c) Timing. First ldg H minus 5 hrs.

7 **Gen Outline**
   (a) The capture of the brs will be a coup de main op depending largely on surprise, speed and dash for success.
   (b) Provided the bulk of your force lands safely, you should have little difficulty in overcoming the known opposition on the brs.
   (c) Your difficulties will arise in holding off an enemy counter-attack on the brs, until you are relieved.

8 Possible enemy counter-attack

    (a) You must expect a counter-attack any time after H minus 4.

    (b) This attack may take the form of a Battle gp consisting of one coy inf in lorries, up to 8 tks and one or two guns mounted on lorries, or it may be a lorried inf coy alone, or inf on foot.

    (c) The most likely line of approach for this force is down one of the rds leading from the WEST or SW, but a cross-country route cannot be ignored.

9 Org of def posn

It is vital that the crossing places be held, and to do this you will secure a close brhead on the WEST bank, in addition to guarding the brs. The immediate def of the brs and of the WEST bank of the canal must be held at all costs.

10 Patrolling

    (a) You will harass and delay the deployment of the enemy counter-attack forces of 736 GR by offensive patrols covering all rd approaches from the WEST. Patrols will remain mobile and offensive.

    (b) Up to one third of your effective force may be used in this role. The remaining two thirds will be used for static def and immediate counter-attack.

Emp of RE

11   (a) You will give to your Sprs the following tasks only, in order of priority:-

            Neutralising the demolition mechanisms.

            Removing charges from demolition chambers.

            Establishing personnel ferries.

    (b) In your detailed planning of the op you will consult the CRE or RE comd nominated by him in the carrying out of these tasks by the RE personnel under your comd.

12 Relief

I estimate that your relief will NOT be completed until H minus 3 hrs, ie, two hrs after your first ldg. One coy 7 Para Bn will, however, be despatched to your assistance with the utmost possible speed after the ldg of the Bn. They should reach your posn by H minus 3 hrs 30 mins, and will come under your comd until arrival of OC 7 Para Bn as in para 13(b).

INTERCOMN

13 (a) You will arrange for an offr or senior NCO to meet CO of 7 Para Bn near their Bn RV at H minus 4 hrs 30 mins with the following infn:-

    (i)   are brs securely held?

    (ii)   are brs intact?

    (iii)   are you in contact with enemy, and if so where, and in what strength?

    (iv)   if brs are blown, state of ferries?

    (v)   where is your coy HQ?

In addition you will give a pre-arranged sig from the brs, to show that they are in your possession, about H minus 4 hrs 15 mins.

(b) OC 7 Para Bn will take over comd of the brhead and of your force on his arrival at the EAST br.

MISC

14 **Glider Loads**

(a) Outline

    Gliders 1–4.   One rifle pl less handcart.
                     5 Sprs.

    Gliders 5–6.   one rifle pl less handcart.
                     5 men Coy HQ.

(b) Detailed Load Tables will be worked out by you in conjunc with the RE and Bde Loading Offr.

15 **Trg**

The trg of your force will be regarded as a first priority matter. Demands for special stores and trg facilities will be sent in through your Bn HQ to HQ 6 Airldg Bde. Until further notice all orders and instrs to you on trg will either originate from or pass through HQ 6 Airldg Bde.

Both Bde HQ will give you every possible help.

NIGEL POETT
Brig.
APO ENGLAND.   Comd 5 Para Bde

Acknowledgements

I wish I could think of an adequate way to express my thanks to every person I interviewed for their hospitality and helpfulness. Without exception, I was welcomed into homes, always offered a meal and/or a drink, frequently invited to spend the night. In the process of doing two dozen interviews in England, I got to see a great deal of the country, which was fun, and to see a great deal of the British people, which was fascinating. I stayed with old-age pensioners, with successful businessmen, with solicitors, on grand country estates, in East End flats, in fashionable West End town houses. D Company, I came to realise, came from every part of British society, with each part making its own contribution to the organisation as a whole. But what impressed me most was the tangible evidence of what good use these men and women had made of the freedom they helped to preserve for themselves and for us on June 6, 1944.

Their friendliness towards me, an unknown Yank prying into their past, I shall never forget. It has been a great privilege and pleasure to have had the opportunity to meet these men and women and to listen to their stories.

Adam Sisman, my editor, provided enthusiasm, energy, and exceptional efficiency, all of which was gratefully and profitably received.

I would also like to thank the University of New Orleans and the Board of Supervisors of the LSU System. In the autumn of 1983 the Board granted me a sabbatical leave, which made it possible for my wife and me to live in London and travel on the Continent, and in Canada, doing the interviews. Without that sabbatical, there would be no book. My gratitude to the University of New Orleans and the Board is deep and permanent.

150

Acknowledgements

My wife, Moira Buckley Ambrose, carried her share of the load with her usual aplomb. As always, she worked hard with me and for me; as always, without her it would not have happened.

Sources

My information on Private Helmut Romer comes from a note Romer sent John Howard, from a POW camp, in late 1945. Private Vern Bonck's story I got from Wally Parr, Major Schmidt's from various British, German and French sources. Georges Gondrée left a written account of his activities. Lieutenant Werner Kortenhaus kindly wrote me an eight-page letter on his experiences; I want to thank Scotty Hirst for putting me in touch with Kortenhaus.

John Howard very kindly lent me all his notes, diaries, photographs, orders and intelligence reports. Jim Wallwork let me make a copy of his written report on operation Deadstick.

I read all the standard books. The ones I found most helpful were Napier Crookenden, *Dropzone Normandy*; General Richard Gale's *Call to Arms* and *6th Division in Normandy*; the official account of the British airborne divisions, entitled *By Air to Battle*; Sir Huw Wheldon, *Red Berets Into Normandy*; Milton Dank, *The Glider Gang*; Hilary Saunders, *The Red Beret*; Barry Gregory, *British Airborne Troops*; James Mrazek, *Fighting Gliders of World War II*; David Howarth, *Dawn of D-Day*; Cornelius Ryan, *The Longest Day*; and Michael Hickey, *Out of the Sky*.

Index

153

Index